The Beauty of Worship

By William Bay

Mel Bay
Pacific, MO
63069-0066

MEL BAY PUBLICATIONS, INC. • PACIFIC, MO. 63069-0066

CONTENTS

PRELUDE

Many scholarly books have been written on the subject of worship. Quite a few have come forth in the past several years. This book, I believe, has a different emphasis. I have undertaken this task with a fervent desire to instill a lasting hunger and thirst for experiencing increasingly more of the presence of God. In addition, I have sought to encourage those who are hesitant, to exhort and build up those who are attempting to walk in faith, and to share a vision of the Church of Jesus Christ. The vision is of a church that affirms and proclaims the glory of God, reigns with power and truth in a darkly troubled world, and which is truly able to reach out to those who yearn for meaning and hope with a love so pervasive and powerful that it completely transcends human understanding.

"Gather My saints together unto Me, those who have made a covenant with Me by sacrifice."   Psalm 50:5

"I will sing unto the Lord as long as I live; I will sing praise to my God while I have my being.

May my meditation of Him be pleasing; I shall be glad in the Lord."   Psalm 104:33-34

Moreover, these pages present a statement by one who deeply loves the Lord and who earnestly seeks true fellowship and unity in the Body of Christ. I long for the day when this Body is knit together totally under the Lordship of Christ, drawing strength and sustenance from journeying together into the holy presence of God, loving and serving each other in humility and joy, and boldly bearing witness to the glorious majesty of God. This is a message for those who seek . . . for those who have ears to hear and eyes to see.

I feel that God is moving today in dynamic and sovereign ways. The Holy Spirit is manifestly present and the standard of our risen Savior is being lifted up. What an exciting time to be alive!

[All scriptures are from the King James version, unless otherwise noted. In several instances the author has used the modern tense of a verb or pronoun. Scriptures marked (NIV) are from the *New International Version,* ©1978 by New York International Bible Society, published by The Zondervan Corporation, Grand Rapids, Michigan 49506.]

Chapter 1

BEGINNINGS

Giving thanks unto the Father, who has made us able to be partakers of the inheritance of the saints in light: Who has delivered us from the power of darkness, and has translated us into the kingdom of His dear Son: Colossians 1:12-13

Images . . . I continually marvel at the vivid mental pictures that remain planted indelibly in our memory. How peculiar it is that we remember some things so clearly and forget others. Yet, there is a pattern woven into our lives, a common thread winding through various ages and events which speaks of a Divine hand . . . a beckoning, a call.

It was Christmas Eve and I was 17 years old. How clearly I remember. Why I went I do not recall, but at 11:30 p.m. I found myself wandering into a Christmas Eve service. At that period in my life I did not allow much room or time for God. I was totally immersed in a flurry of goals, activities, and ambitions. There I was, walking into the sanctuary . . . late. People were standing, it was dark, and I quietly slid into the outside end of a pew near the back of the church. Suddenly, I looked around and started noticing things that seemed wonderfully strange. People were holding candles and a soft, radiant, beautiful glow filled the room. As I looked I noticed a peaceful joy on the faces of many. I also had the peculiar feeling of being totally unnoticed. It was as though I was viewing something holy, something totally set apart from the world of my experience and yet, I stood aside as an onlooker, an observer. My ears picked up the soft, heavenly sound of voices singing . . . voices filling the air, everywhere.

Silent night, holy night! All is calm, all is bright. Round yon Virgin mother and Child, Holy Infant so tender and mild, Sleep in heavenly peace, Sleep in heavenly peace.

And the glorious, gentle sound continued . . .

Silent night, holy night! Son of God, love's pure light, Radiant beams from Thy holy face, With the dawn of redeeming grace: Jesus, Lord, at Thy birth, Jesus, Lord, at Thy birth.

I turned around and glanced anxiously. What was happening? Were others also feeling and seeing something strangely wonderful? Was this the way it always was? Did they know? Could they tell me? I left that service filled with questions and wonder. It was like being in a dream where after years and years of searching, you wandered into a beautiful, peaceful setting and somehow knew that you were home at last. Still, I agonized over the questions. "How can this be?" "Why?" Many years passed before those questions found answers.

Another clear memory . . . this one pivotal in the pattern my life would take. It was 1971. I will never forget. I had accompanied my sister to Barnes Hospital in St. Louis where her husband lay dying of cancer. As we walked down the long sterile corridor, we were greeted by a grim-faced doctor who said that he believed Bill, my brother-in-law, would last only a few more hours. My sister turned to me and said that she wished to spend the next several hours alone with her husband. "Is there anything I can do?", I asked feebly. She thought a moment and then said, "Yes, there is." I watched numbly as she reached in her purse, grasped a New Testament, and asked me to read it. Out of obedience to her request I located a quiet, out-of-the-way waiting room and began to read the Gospel of John.

At that moment, time seemed to stand still. Words jumped off of the pages and dug deeply into my heart. It was a dawning of understanding and light. It was the beginning of a new life, a journey. Something in the heavenlies moved that night. My life, in several brief hours, took on incredible new meaning and direction. I was not the only one that night who received a touch of the Master's hand. Bill began a startling and dramatic recovery. God, at that moment and in that dark little hospital room, began leading him on a miraculous journey of faith and grace. The events of that evening will be emblazoned on my memory forever.

Images . . . As I reflect on that evening and on events and places since, I recall a recurring theme of yearning to enter God's presence mixed with a longing to be there with God's people. Another vivid picture comes to mind. It was a balmy spring day and I was in a state park in Georgia. I entered into a little stone chapel and began to pray. Once again, time seemed to stand still. As I prayed, I felt as if the veil separating me from eternity was ever so gently lifted. God was so near! I have no idea how long I remained in that quiet little chapel. I do remember not wanting to leave. There is such tranquility and peace in God's presence. Once we begin to enter His gates, our fullest desire is to remain, to linger.

There have been so many images and reflections. Some years ago I was in California attending a Christian conference being held in a large church. The activities of the evening had ended, but I remained seated in a quiet corner of the sanctuary. Quite a number of young people had also stayed. They had experienced something special and they did not want to leave. Once again, God seemed so near. I think we all sensed it. As we continued to pray and worship, young people started coming into the sanctuary. I do not know exactly where they came from. Most simply wandered in from the street. The next thing I recall was the sound of a beautiful melody rising spontaneously from all present and the sight of scores of young people, drug culture and all, kneeling and weeping all over the front of the church. As I looked I saw what seemed like a sea of people, arm-in-arm and hand-in-hand, sharing in God's presence. Tears . . . yes. Tears of brokenness. Tears of joy. Tears of love and compassion.

Another image that stirs in my memory is of a darkened church on a cold winter night. My wife and I belonged to a small prayer group. The sister of one member was to undergo serious brain surgery on the next day. We were interceding in prayer on her behalf through the night. I entered the church around 2:00 a.m. and met another man in our prayer group. He was getting ready to leave. It was near Christmas and we sat briefly and looked together at the Gospel of Luke. For a precious few minutes we reflected on the wondrous story of Christ's birth.

After my friend left, I went inside the small chapel and began to read out of the book of Psalms. The book of Psalms always speaks to me in very meaningful ways. (Oh, how I love David's spirit!) After reading a while, I knelt and began to pray. There, in the wee hours of that cold night, in the dimly lit, quiet chapel, God again seemed so close . . . so very near. It was as though the gentle, loving presence of the Holy Spirit was filling the room. I cannot help but wonder how incredible eternity must be, living forever in the Divine presence.

Finally, I reflect on a summer evening in a wood chapel in Colorado. A community of Christians had gathered to worship and my wife, children, and I were visiting. The air was crisp and the smell of incense mixed with the aroma of pine. The songs were gentle. Jesus was being glorified as many voices, blending as one, joined in spontaneous prayer and song. "Jesus, what a wonder You are!" There, once again, I could feel God saying, "Look! See! . . . There is a calling I have for my people . . . an experience and sharing of each other's lives, so rich, so full. Can you really see it? Do you hear? It is not for just some. It is My will for all. If My people would only hearken unto Me. I desire to be among them. I desire to be with them . . . rejoicing with them on the glorious mountain peaks . . . leading them in love through the valleys. Will you see? Will you hear?"

I pray earnestly that my words, thoughts, and feelings expressed on these pages will somehow begin to lift the veil for you. That they will encourage and help you to draw close . . . to catch the glorious vision of what life can and should be in God's presence . . . as we share Him together.

"Let us draw near with a true heart in full assurance of faith, having our hearts sprinkled from an evil conscience, and our bodies washed with pure water."
Hebrews 10:22

Chapter 2

EXPERIENCING GOD

"O God, Thou art my God, early will I seek Thee; my soul thirsts for Thee, my flesh longs for Thee in a dry and thirsty land, where no water is, To see Thy power and Thy glory, as I have seen Thee in the sanctuary."

Psalm 63:1-2

Do you believe that God really wants us to experience His presence? Do you believe that He desires to fellowship with us? Do you know that He longs to have lasting communion with you? These are staggering yet wonderful thoughts. Is this an experience for a select few spiritual experts? God forbid! Is being in the presence of God a common experience realized in the lives of most Christians? Tragically not! Why? Perhaps it stems from the busyness of modern life.

We are so busy that we seem to have time for very little, yet weeks and months go by and we wonder, "What have I done with my time?" If you do not believe that we are locked into a furious pace of life that makes us slaves to endless activities and schedules, try eliminating things in order to simplify your schedule! Incredible, isn't it? Do we have time for God? What a peculiar state of affairs. Here we have the Creator of the universe, the Living God saying, "Draw near, Come into My presence, Learn of Me, I will refresh your souls." And yet, we do not have the time or ability to become "uncluttered." We have to desperately desire to experience God's presence and then we need to learn how to go about doing it.

I remember hearing of a minister who felt a real hunger and thirst for more of God. He and a beloved Christian brother would set aside one night of the week and meet in the sanctuary of his church. Frequently, the only lighting used was several candles. They would sit on the floor or wherever seemed comfortable and would pray and focus all of their thoughts on God in His glory. Sometimes they would wait or pray silently for long periods. Sometimes they would break into joyous song or spontaneous prayer. At other moments they would read or recite scripture. Their only agenda was adoring God and waiting on Him. They were learning to sit at His feet and listen to the gentle voice of the Holy Spirit.

What infinite blessing it is to rest in the Lord, to drink deeply of His waters, to receive His Divine refreshing, to abandon ourselves in praise and adoration, to break into glory! Strange thoughts? Perhaps a little weird? Tragically, we exist in an age that says, "Live for the moment." "Experience life to the fullest!" (Apart from God, that is.) Yet, society cooly demands that God be experienced in a detached, cerebral way. "We do live in a scientific age, you know." "Emotions, at least in your religious faith, are out!" All the while society attempts to define, limit, and even experience God only in terms of rational reason and intellect, the voice of God continues to say to us, "Draw near. Come unto me." Yes, God wants us to experience Him in continuously deeper ways.

"Oh, taste and see that the Lord is good; blessed is the man who trusts in Him."   *Psalm 34:8*

"Delight thyself also in the Lord, and He shall give thee the desires of thine heart."   *Psalm 37:4*

We live in an age of "Marthas." (Luke 10:38-42) People are busy and preoccupied with endless activities and tasks. Many of these are quite necessary, worthwhile, and even righteous. Nevertheless, this hectic pace either prevents us from spending time with God or wears us out to such an extent that we are too tired to hear, see, or experience anything. Spiritually speaking, God wants "Marys." As found in the story in Luke's Gospel, these are the people who worship at the Lord's feet. They seek Him and they adore

Him. They devote quality time to worshipping Him even if there is cost involved. (We always have lots of important things to do!) In the words of Anne Ortlund, "The world says, 'Don't just stand there, do something.' Christ says, 'Don't just do something, stand there!'"[1]

The fragmentation of modern life is another reason why we have such difficulty experiencing God. We live in a troubled and broken world. A gnawing depression and fear haunt us because for all of our intellectual prowess, economic advantages, and "sophisticated" secular mores, we dwell in realms of isolation and loneliness. We feel alienated, alone, insignificant, and scared. Yet society offers us the bitterest remedy of all. "Do your own thing." "Be somebody!" "Learn to achieve by using the latent powers of your mind . . . you can do it all." The prevailing secular treatments lead to more sickness.

Like the misguided medical "experts" of old, the ringing prophets of our secular age seek to stop the hemorrhaging by letting more blood! If we are fortunate enough to hop off of this frantic merry-go-round called "The Good Life" and "Enlightened Liberation," we might hear the voice of Jesus softly saying, "He who loses his life, shall gain it." What a strange thought for modern man. (We have come a long way, . . . haven't we?) Strangely, this poignant message of Christ is the only cure for the destructive spiral of self gratification and indulgence. Having a heart desirous of laying down self interest, ambition, and actualization in order to reach out to others with Jesus' love and to help them stand, walk, cope, survive, triumph . . . being able, at a sacrificial cost, to enable

[1]Anne Ortlund, *Up With Worship,* (Glendale: Regal Books, Gospel Light Publisher, 1975) p. 58.

another to succeed and then to rejoice in their success, . . . this is real love. This is freedom. This is life!

There is just something about discovering the reality and presence of God that makes all of those desires and ambitions for which we have clawed and scraped seem to pass peacefully away. Knowing Jesus gives our lives dramatic new perspective. Christianity was never meant to be a comfortable religion. It was meant to be a radical, life transforming call. Perhaps the Church has become too "respectable." People throughout the world search diligently for causes and ideals to live and die for. The Kingdom of God is meaning and life! What poor, misguided, hollow substitutes the world grasps. May we never shrink from loudly proclaiming the dynamic truth and tremendous power of the gospel. May the focus of our lives be intent and unwavering on the Kingdom of God.

Jesus said, "The kingdom of heaven is like treasure hidden in a field. When a man found it, he hid it again, and then in his joy went and sold all he had and bought that field.

Again, the kingdom of heaven is like a merchant looking for fine pearls. When he found one of great value, he went away and sold everything he had and bought it."

Matthew 13:44-46 (NIV)

Oh Lord, place in each of our hearts a burning desire and zeal for You and Your kingdom. Let us seek You with absolutely all of our hearts, souls, minds, and bodies!

"But seek ye first the kingdom of God, and his righteousness, and all these things shall be added unto you." — Matthew 6:33

Chapter 3

WORSHIP, THE SUMMIT OF OUR EXISTENCE

"And the Spirit and the bride say, Come. And let him that heareth say, Come. And let him that is athirst come. And whosoever will, let him take the water of life freely." Revelation 22:17

Worship is the primary function of our lives. It is the wellspring of our existence. All of history culminates in a glorious scene of worship. Both the end of our existence and the purpose throughout are involved intimately with worshipping God.

"This shall be written for the generation to come; and the people who shall be created shall praise the Lord." Psalm 102:18

In addition, worship has always been the response of God's people to His sovereign presence and power in their lives. (Luke 1:46-55, Ezra 3:11,1 Samuel 2:1-10, Genesis 35:13-15, etc.) The Risen Christ, the Alpha and Omega, speaks with power and finality when He says, "Worship God." (Revelation 22:10)

When we learn to come together in worship, God's love is shed in and through us, His grace is bestowed upon us, and His power is manifested among us. Giving our lives to worship gives vitality and freshness to our very existence. To the extent that we yield to that Divine urging within us, we allow God's sun to shine through and cleanse the very core of our being. Giving our hearts and souls to worship allows us to continually discover God in new and deeper ways. It allows us to become one with each other in a magnificent vision of God's eternal glory and purposes. We begin to witness internally that we are part of something exceedingly wonderful that somehow transcends our comprehension. We are part of the eternal Family of God! We are joined by the deep bonds of Christ together with all the saints in heaven and on earth.

Giving ourselves to worship and abandoning our spirits and souls to adoration of God and to His love expressed toward each other allows us to dream dreams and to hope for the future. It creates a vibrant, expectant atmosphere where God's majesty and our innermost yearnings meet in glorious union, resulting in vision . . . both personal and corporate. In worship we bow before the sovereignty of the True and Living King. We give glory and honor to His name. Some out of hearts filled with joy and triumph, . . . others out of hearts heavy with sadness, suffering, or want. Yet, the Lord transcends all of these circumstances, attitudes, feelings, and conditions and lifts us, from wherever we are, to a higher plateau of sharing His presence . . . resulting in continually firmer ground on which to place steps of faith on our journey called obedience to God, the new life in Christ! God seeks and desires worshippers. (John 4:23) Oh, that we would hear His voice!

"For with Thee is the fountain of life; in Thy light we shall see light."   *Psalm 36:9*

What then is worship? I must confess that the subject is so pervasive, so deep, and so broad that many writers grapple unmercifully with the attempt to define it. There is an old saying about "trying to light a candle" rather than "trying to fill a bucket." I think that I would prefer to light candles. Actually, so much of our lives as Christians is intimately involved with worship that I sincerely feel the necessity to set broad guidelines, rooted in truth, which encourage others to partake! To me, worship concerns the deepest level of our relationships with God and with each other and how the extent, strength, and quality of these relationships find expression in action. It is attributing worth to God, bringing glory, laud, and honor to His name by all of the actions we take, both direct and indirect.

Worship, you see, is more than just singing songs or praying prayers. It concerns what we do on Sunday mornings at various places, but is not limited to times, places, or certain specific activities. Worship originates with God. He plants a Divine hunger in us to draw near, experience His presence, and thereby break into glorious adoration and praise. Worship involves the condition of our heart. It is from the heart that we respond to that Divine urging. A heart hungry for God is a fantastic blessing. Not only is our heart hungry, it is filled with expectancy. We worship God with an expectant faith, knowing that He seeks our fellowship and inhabits our praise.

> *"But without faith it is impossible to please Him; for he that comes to God must believe that He is, and that He is a rewarder of them that diligently seek Him."* — *Hebrews 11:6*

One of the blessed aspects of worship is the intimate fellowship with our Heavenly Father which we enter through prayer. By so doing, we are able to bare our innermost being . . . our love, our hopes, our fears, our anger, our anxiety, our joy, our dreams . . . with the Lord and Giver of Life. He is the only One who really knows us to the core of our soul, the One who knows exactly who we are . . . and yet, who loves us deeply, gently, sacrificially, peacefully, infinitely . . . who wants only the very best for us and who has a perfectly unique plan for our lives which, when realized and followed in obedience and faith, brings us into a calling of inner peace, joy, and service which fulfills our deepest longings and glorifies God.

Worship, also, must be based on truth. While it relates to our attitudes toward God and our inner revelation of His personality, character, and attributes, those attitudes and revelations must be true and accurate.

"God is a Spirit: and they that worship Him must worship Him in spirit and truth."

John 4:24

God is not merely who or what we desire Him to be. God is revealed in His word. Our understanding of Him must rest on the clear revelation of scripture. However, as we become worshippers and devote our hearts increasingly to worship, we can expect continuously deeper perceptions and revelations within various contexts. For example, scripture reveals that God is merciful. The longer we walk with God, the longer we share His life with our brothers and sisters in Christ, the fuller will be our understanding of God's mercy. We learn from scripture that God is just. It takes a lifetime of learning of God, walking with Him, and sharing Him with others before we start to gain full comprehension of what His justice completely entails.

Both the depth and the extent of our personal relationship with God are crucial. How deep is our water? We need to answer this question honestly. Whenever I meet someone who truly seeks God with an open and sincere heart, I know I have met someone ready to enter into genuine worship.

"Blessed are they who do hunger and thirst after righteousness; for they shall be filled."

Matthew 5:6

23

How sad it is that we sometimes allow religion to implant a feeling of "arrival," a feeling that says, "I am in good standing in my church, I am a good and righteous person, and I have all that I need!" God delights in filling hungry hearts and in quenching spiritual thirst.

". . . open thy mouth wide, and I will fill it."
Psalm 81:10

If complacency and general apathy mark our hearts and attitudes, our worship will be dull, routine, and lifeless.

While worship depends largely on our relationship to God, it also depends greatly on the extent and quality of our relationships with each other. This is such a vital area and yet we so frequently interact in shallow terms. When we use the word "fellowship," what do we mean? Are we talking merely about a brief 15 minute coffee hour after church? Are we referring to rather safe and guarded conversations at the men's meeting, ladies' luncheon, or rummage sale?

God is calling us to drastically rethink the depth of relationships we have in the Body of Christ. This is both an essential and serious matter. There is great risk in deepening our relationships. By getting close, we allow others to learn of our hopes, our failures, our fears and anxieties, our weaknesses, and even our strengths. Can we trust them? Many have proved to be untrustworthy. Nevertheless, it is worth the risk. Removing the "masks" and sharing caring, compassionate love with others is a blessed experience. Remember, there always is a cost to bear in becoming a true worshipper. God both expects us to pay that price and promises to honor our obedience as we act out His will by faith.

A few years ago my wife and I began meeting with a small group of friends to study scripture and to "fellowship." At the beginning, none of us thought seriously about our relationships. It was not long, though, before we began to realize that God was expanding our understanding of the bonds that hold together the Body of Christ. It has been a long process, highlighted by sunny peaks and some rather dark valleys, but several of us have sincerely felt a "fusing process" taking place in our lives and families. Believe me, when Christians go through suffering and trials together, their worship draws from deep bonds. It is out of these bonds of fellowship that we hear Christ say, "There I am in the midst of you," in an increasingly powerful way. It is worth the cost! Worship springs from love. True love, however, is based on truth, requires understanding and compassion, and demands sacrifice. Love is not cheap. It is, however, infinitely glorious if it is encountered with brothers and sisters in bonds of costly unity and expressed together in adoration of God!

While the level of our worship is conditioned by our walk with God and with each other, it has another side. We must never lose sight of the fact that God is sovereign. His grace transcends our full understanding. I heard a man say once that he had always found a degree of mystery in God. (And this man was a gifted teacher of scripture.) No matter how iron-clad our theology is, we must never forget that God is larger than our intellect and there are things concerning Him that we may never fully comprehend until we see Him "face to face." This should give us great comfort. Realizing this begins to open our eyes of faith to an incredible vista of God's grace working in our lives. Acknowledging that, try as we might, we can never keep God trapped in intellectual or theological boxes, gives Him genuine room to work. We suddenly are filled with a spirit of expectancy.

"But Jesus beheld them, and said unto them, 'With men this is impossible, but with God all things are possible.'
Matthew 19:26

In regard to worship we must acknowledge that as we freely give ourselves to worshipping God, God draws us close to Him. He takes our open hearts and deepens the relationship. Also, as we sincerely yield ourselves in worship with others, we are granted deeper bonds of love, understanding, and trust. Therefore, the very act and practice of worship builds and strengthens our relationships with God and with our brothers and sisters in Christ! God is wondrous and merciful, isn't He! In my own life, I have grown so much in love for others and in communion with God through worship experiences. His well is deep, His river is broad, and His waters are pure! Remember this! We cannot immerse ourselves in God's waters by merely listening to someone eloquently telling us how wonderful and deep they are. We have to get in the water ourselves! God has not called us to be hearers, He has called us to be doers. Faith needs action. Belief requires obedience.

"But be ye doers of the word and not hearers only, deceiving your own selves."
James 1:23

Chapter 4

THE NECESSITY AND BLESSINGS OF WORSHIP

"And all these blessings shall come on thee, and overtake thee, if thou shalt hearken unto the voice of the Lord thy God."

Deuteronomy 28:2

Worship is necessary to survive. If we allow ourselves to worship God in a complacent and feeble manner, our Christian lives will lack power and strength. If we worship a false picture or understanding of God, we will lead Christian lives misdirected and tragically out of balance. Also, if we go so far as to worship false gods (our sophisticated modern world offers a wealth of idols—religious, secular, political), our lives will lack fulfillment. In this latter event, despair and emptiness will likely be the fruit which we bear. Many of these areas will be expanded upon later in this text. Suffice it to say that healthy, vibrant worship, which is bursting with joyous life and which is based on true understanding of who God is, what He is like, and what His will for us is, leads to strong Christian lives brimming with vitality and zeal.

Worship serves as a sign to the world. It is a testimony to God's reality and presence. Who can forget the wonder and excitement on the day of Pentecost when the multitudes heard the apostles praising the works of God in various tongues. Worship should say to the world in a bold way, "God is alive! He rules the heavens and the earth! He is here!" What picture does the world have of God and Christ's Body, the Church, when it views most worship services found today? May our lives, our work, our relationships, our love, and our worship cry out boldly, "Glory!" to God.

There is a rather uneasy mixture between the secular world and the church in the area of worship. The church, especially in the arts, has become a follower of styles, trends, and even statements made in secular circles. We should never lose our feeling of being a unique people, called out of the world, and then sent back into the world with the specific light which shines from the truth and power of the Gospel of the Kingdom.

"for you are a people holy to the Lord your God. Out

of all the peoples on the face of the earth, the Lord has chosen you to be his treasured possession."

Deuteronomy 14:2(NIV)

"Wherefore, come out from among them, and be ye separate, saith the Lord, . . .

2 Corinthians 6:17

This does not mean that we withdraw and become a cloistered group of believers. It does mean, however, that we should reaffirm the uniqueness of our calling. I firmly believe that a strong, glorious church filled with people totally given to worshipping God in spirit and truth will be the leader in society and the arts with inspired truth, revelation, creativity, and innovation. Let us remember that our worship must be directed toward pleasing God and rekindling in us the vision and fire of being God's "peculiar" people. We should never compromise that calling for the sake of expediency or for the purpose of conforming to or pleasing the world. If we try to please the world on its own terms, ultimately it will hold us in contempt. Even worse, we may in fact be offering God a "blemished lamb." God's truth does not need "help" and it does not need to be compromised. His truth brings liberty and strength. Worship that affirms that truth is pleasing to God. In the end, that is what the world will respect.

"And He hath put a new song in my mouth, even praise unto our God; many shall see it and fear, and shall trust in the Lord"   Psalm 40:3

Worship brings spiritual freedom and undergirds spiritual growth. I am always amazed at how guarded we are with our spirituality. When it comes to our relationship with God, we frequently are "pent-up" and bound. It is not clear whether this has resulted from pressures of society or from misguided religious tradition. Probably, it has resulted from a mixture of both. Let us look back again to David. What an intense, passionate spirit! How often we have heard people say that their faith was "personal" or "private." Often, these same individuals describe worship with adjectives like "decent, orderly, or controlled."

Fair enough. But, let us never hold God at arms length. Would we dare describe the relationship with our spouse as "decent, orderly, and controlled?" (Tragically, I am certain that many could!) Let us develop a spirit of openness. This is a spirit that longs for free flowing communion with God. It is a spirit which dares to say to our Creator, "Let me draw close to You. Let me learn of You. Let me love You."

I used to be quite inhibited. In fact, I was an extreme case. I remember going to prayer meetings with my sister and wondering secretly as I left the house if the neighbors knew where I was going! Talk about being "reserved." Just mustering up enough boldness to stick a Christian bumper sticker on my car was a terrific spiritual battle. (Of course it was a nice conservative "sign of the fish." Nothing so flamboyant as "Honk if you love Jesus." Mercy!) If we really are seeking God with sincere hearts, He has a way of "freeing us up."

I remember that, back then, whenever I went to a prayer meeting or worship service, I always subconsciously tried to find a quiet, unobtrusive place to sit. It seemed, however, that I always managed to end up next to someone absolutely bubbling with joy and "liberty" in the spirit. In addition, these individuals, after taking a good notice of me, frequently felt a calling to share their "freedom" with me. God must have an incredible sense of humor! He must shed both tears of laughter and pain at our attempts to worship Him on our own terms. In my own life I have learned that, to the extent with which we allow our hearts, minds, and bodies to freely break forth in worship, we will experience an inward loosening, a breaking of "fetters," a cracking of our "plaster spiritual cast." The result is joy, edification, and real inner tranquility. It is ultimately a decision of our will. Will we allow ourselves to worship? Will we openly praise God? Will we abandon our lives to His Lordship?

Worship also builds and enriches the life of our Christian family. It increases the vitality of our community. If we worship regularly with people, we cannot help but grow closer to them. There are, however, several notable exceptions. If we choose to participate in worship, hermetically sealed in our private little "alabaster vases," we cannot experience much drawing together. Once again, many people do choose to remain isolated, forgoing the fullness of the worship experience, in order to preserve the privacy of their personality. (That's really no fun, folks!) We can also miss the boat if our worship is dead, lifeless, or misdirected. It really is tragic to settle for less than the best that God offers.

Several years ago I was flying home from a business trip. It was a rather long flight. I was sitting next to an elderly black lady who was reading some sort of prayer book. I have never been really big on airplane conversation so after a few pleasantries, I opened a current Christian book and proceeded to read for most of the flight. I did notice that she looked over occasionally to see what I was reading. As the plane landed and rolled to a stop, I turned and gave her a cordial, "Good-by." She looked straight at me and said with deep sincerity, "May God bless you, Bill."

Something inside of me suddenly felt crushed. It was as though, in her few brief parting words, I had realized that there was a true bond between us. That bond was Jesus. Because of my general reserved nature and my preoccupied frame of mind, I had missed a God given opportunity to share something meaningful and eternal with another. I definitely felt that God was grieved.

Why do so many of us try to partake of God's ocean of love and fellowship with only a thimble? Someday I expect to meet that wonderful lady in heaven. Believe me, then we shall share!

The point is this: If we are willing to open ourselves to others and share the love that God is creating in us, the fellowship will be beautiful, and lasting bonds will emerge. Dynamic worship effectively breaks down barriers and builds love and trust. In addition, worship provides the arena where love is practiced and taught. How grateful I am for worship and for other hungry Christians with which to share it.

Worship also provides a pivotal setting where vision can be received. As the Psalmist said, "In thy light we shall see light." Vision is essential to life.

"Where there is no vision, the people perish . . ."
Proverbs 29:18

This is so very important. Have we ever given much thought to who we are to be as God's people? We have not merely been called out of the world. We have been called *into* something. What is that *something* to be?

"For thou art a holy people unto the Lord thy God; the Lord thy God hath chosen thee to be a special people unto himself, above all people who are upon the face of the earth."

Deuteronomy 7:6

"But you are a chosen generation, a royal priesthood, a holy nation, a people of His own, that you should show forth the praises of Him who has called you out of darkness into His marvelous light;"

1 Peter 2:9

What does the Body of Christ look like to us? Where is it going? Or perhaps, where should it be going? Where is our particular fellowship or church in that picture? Where do we individually fit into that Body? Are we in some way contributing to the building up or equipping of the Body? All of these questions are vital. What precious few moments we spend reflecting on them.

You see, we are all on a journey to a city whose builder and maker is God! Have we really internalized that fact? Are we groping blindly or do we see a clear light leading us, revealing God's will? Worship allows us to dwell in God's presence. It develops a sensitivity to Him. It continually opens our eyes to God's sovereign power and grace working in the lives of His saints. It opens the door to vision. We gain a sense of purpose and we begin to see more accurately. We are changed "from glory to glory." (2 Corinthians 3:18)

"Beloved, now are we the children of God, and it does not yet appear what we shall be, but we know that, when He shall appear, we shall be like Him; for we shall see Him as He is."

1 John 3:2

Who can forget the words of the Apostle John when before his eyes unfolded the fantastic vision of the culmination of history and God in glory?

"I was in the Spirit on the Lord's day . . .

Revelation 1:10

Yes, as we enter into worship we begin to see. As with John, vision frequently arises out of worship.

Another important aspect of worship is that it kindles in us a desire for holiness. God is holy!

"And the four living creatures had each of them six wings about him, and they were full of eyes within; and they rest not day and night, saying, Holy, holy holy, Lord God Almighty, who was, and is, and is to come."

Revelation 4:8

As we see God more clearly, our sinfulness becomes more painfully apparent and we earnestly desire cleansing. Note the response of Isaiah when he saw the Lord.

" . . . I saw the Lord sitting upon a throne, high and lifted up, and His train filled the temple.

Above it stood the seraphim: each one had six wings; with two he covered his face, and with two he covered his feet, and with two he did fly.

And one cried unto another, and said, Holy, holy, holy is the Lord of hosts; the whole earth is full of His glory.

And the posts of the door moved at the voice of him who cried, and the house was filled with smoke.

Then said I, 'Woe is me! For I am undone, because I am a man of unclean lips, and I dwell in the midst of a people of unclean lips; for mine eyes have seen the King, the Lord of hosts."

Isaiah 6:1-5

Try closing your eyes and reflecting on that passage. Truly, there is beauty and awe in holiness.

"Oh, worship the Lord in the beauty of holiness;"
Psalms 96:9

As we give our hearts and souls in worship to God, we are flooded with an intense desire to repent of our sinfulness and to be purified so that nothing stands in the way or hinders our experience of God. Remember, God demands holiness in His people.

> *"Speak unto all the congregation of the children of Israel, and say unto them, 'You shall be holy; for I, the Lord your God, am holy."*
>
> Leviticus 19:2

Jesus also indicated that we cannot see God without a cleansing and a purity of heart.

> *"Blessed are the pure in heart; for they shall see God."*
>
> Matthew 5:8

Experiencing the presence of God is both awesome and transforming. As Moses came down from Mount Sinai and the presence of God, his face shone so brightly that Aaron and the children of Israel were afraid. (Exodus 34:29-30) In fact, Moses had to wear a veil because his face radiated so! May we come to glow like that!

> *"You are the light of the world . . ."*
>
> Matthew 5:14(NIV)

When giving workshops on worship, I am always overjoyed at the gradual change in facial expressions as the session develops. Often in the beginning expressions are very stiff, guarded, and reserved. After a period of sharing and participation, faces start glowing! A happiness and joy begins to pervade the room, and some tears even start to flow. As the people sing and praise God, their countenances reflect a definite step taken, no matter how small, closer to the living God.

Another important aspect of worship is that it provides an essential basis for all ministry and outreach. If our lives are filled with the presence of God, the Divine fragrance will radiate on everything we touch, and on everyone we meet. As we grow upward in devotion to God and inward in love for each other, united and strengthened by the powerful bonds of worship, it is only natural for us to flow outward in ministry to those in need. To fail to do so leads to a cloistered mentality and a drying up or a distortion of the Spirit's presence. In my own experience, I have found that real, Spirit-filled worship is the best evangelism program available! People are desperately hungry for God. They may be fighting that fact or they may have allowed the world to temporarily blind them; but nevertheless, when they see people worshipping a living, loving God who "Is Here," they are touched and moved. Dynamic worship bears much fruit!

Growing together as a family in and through worship paves the way for outreach. It would be helpful to re-read the first several chapters of the book of Acts. Notice especially that the Apostles gathered together "in one accord." And the result? The Spirit fell. Farther along we read,

> "And they continued steadfastly in the apostles' doctrine and fellowship, and in breaking of bread, and in prayers."   Acts 2:42

Continuing,

> "And they, continuing daily with one accord in the temple, and breaking bread from house to house, did eat their food with gladness and singleness of heart,

Praising God, and having favor with all the people. And the Lord added to the church daily such as should be saved."   *Acts 2:46-47*

Is it any wonder that it was later said of them that they had "turned the world upside down?" (Acts 17:6) In more recent history we think of the Pilgrims, gathered together out of common faith and persecution, setting out in faith to fulfill a God-given vision. One hundred and two people, crammed for 66 days in a tiny space in the belly of the ship, tossed to and fro on stormy seas, venturing together into the unknown, and guided and nurtured only by faith.

Sometimes God turns up the thermostat to weld us into a people. God can use adversity or persecution, whoever or whatever the cause, to fuse us together. During those times, if we keep our eyes fixed upon the Lord and unite together in sacrificial and costly worship, His transforming love and power is manifested in our midst. How blessed God's presence is in such times! Below is a diagram which pictures some of the facets of worship and the interaction of relationships. This sums up much of what we have been discussing.

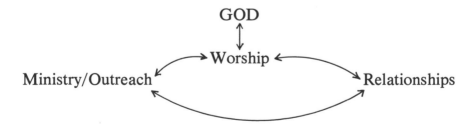

God's power in our midst . . . another glorious aspect of worship. I sincerely believe that we are awakening to something quite significant and that we shall increasingly see tremendous works of God happening in the midst of worshipping Christians. This will not be the ordinary Sunday service as we know it. This will be dynamic, powerful worship. Do we have the faith to worship God with a sense of expectancy and excitement? As we worship, do we feel a sense of Divine linkage with the eternal and of the veil being lifted and heavenly hosts watching? When we worship, are we really "preparing the way of the Lord?" (Luke 3:3-4)

God is present! Give yourselves to Him! . . . Praise and adore Him! . . . Receive His love! . . . Partake of His grace! You see, when our hearts and lives are full of God, there will be a joyous bursting forth of praise and adoration in individual and corporate worship. I believe that God delights to fellowship with us in such settings.

"But Thou art holy, O Thou who inhabitest the praises of Israel."   *Psalm 22:3*

When all of the work that Solomon had made for the house of the Lord was finished, then Solomon brought in the ark, the instrument for the presence of God, and the following events took place.

"It came even to pass, as the trumpeters and singers were as one, to make one sound to be heard in praising and thanking the Lord; and when they lifted up their voice with the trumpets and cymbals and instruments of music, and praised the Lord, saying, For He is good; for His mercy endureth

forever—that then the house was filled with a cloud, even the house of the Lord.

So that the priests could not stand to minister by reason of the cloud; for the glory of the Lord had filled the house of God."

2 Chronicles 5:13-14

Oh, that the glory of the Lord would so fill our gatherings of worship. May the glory of the Lord so fill our lives!

As we progress on our Christian journey, we soon discover that the road has a big sign on it marked "FAITH." We really cannot continue without it. Worship undergirds faith in a very positive manner. As we continually draw near to God in the charged atmosphere of dynamic worship, our love for Him and our understanding of "the God of Scripture" deepens and grows. We learn that He is trustworthy. We witness His sovereign hand in our lives and in the lives of others. We also learn how to humble ourselves and go before Him in times of trial and testing. As we bow down before God in adoration, we hear Him say, "I am with you."

"When you pass through the waters, I will be with you; and through the rivers, they shall not overflow you; when you walk through the fire, you shall not be burned, neither shall the flame kindle upon you." Isaiah 43:2

All of us go through testing and trials where we feel

40

"alone." After knowing God, how frightful it is when we say, "Oh, Lord where are You? Take not your presence from me." But He is near. We are the ones who have strayed. Listen to David's words.

> "For I said in my haste, I am cut off from before Thine eyes; nevertheless, Thou heardest the voice of my supplications when I cried unto Thee."
>
> Psalm 31:22

God is so worthy to be praised! What strength we have in life knowing that He is with us.

> Oh, magnify the Lord with me, and let us exalt His name together.
> I sought the Lord, and He heard me, and delivered me from all my fears."
>
> Psalm 34:3-4

We worship God because He is worthy to be worshipped. By so doing we are able to know Him in very deep and personal ways. Our lives are filled with a dynamic sense of excitement and expectancy. Our faith increases. Scripture reads like loving letters from our God to us, His people. How wonderful it is to venture forth in faith, being led by the Holy Spirit and God's word, and being sustained by fellowship with God, Himself!

Trials are a part of life. We are never promised total freedom from problems. Worship lifts our spirits and enables us to endure and to press on to victory. There is a depth of worship which emerges from ones seeking God in a lonely valley or amidst persecution that cannot be equalled. Perhaps this depth stems from the absolute earnestness with which we seek Him. Out of those experiences we are able to sincerely and joyously affirm:

> ". . . *Weeping may endure for a night, but joy cometh in the morning.*" Psalm 30:5

And,

> "*And we know that all things work together for good to them that love God, to them who are the called according to His purpose.*" Romans 8:28

Jesus is Lord of all of life. He shares His mountain-top glory with us, and He lovingly leads us through those dark valleys we encounter. Once again, worship allows us to "reach out and take His hand."

Several years ago I was going through a severe testing. It was one of those times when God wanted me to stand in faith, but worries, anxieties, and fear were waging a real war inside of me. There were many occasions when I would hike or jog in the woods and use that time to pour out my soul to the Lord in adoration and affirmation of His lordship and power. How the clouds lifted during those moments! In those periods of devotion and worship amidst swirling turbulence, God shed peace and refreshing throughout my being. Worship sustained me. A very strong bond of loving trust emerged from my communion with God. No amount of self effort or mental conditioning could match this bond arising from worship. I came to the place where I was able to state with peace and assurance,

"But I trusted in Thee, O Lord; I said, Thou art my God. My times are in Thy hand; . . ."
Psalm 31:14-15

During this period I was made acutely aware of our tremendous need for brothers and sisters in Christ with whom we can worship freely. There were times when a nagging sense of despair would creep into my spirit. At those times I longed to be with other Christians, united and yielded unto praise and adoration of God. Oh, what a Divine privilege it is to proclaim the power, majesty, and infinite loving kindness of God in the company of His saints. What power is present when we gather together out of passionate hunger for God and love for each other! How greatly God does bless us.

"Oh, how great is Thy goodness, which Thou hast laid up for those who fear Thee, which Thou hast wrought for those who trust in Thee before the sons of men!
Oh, love the Lord, all ye His saints; for the Lord preserveth the faithful, and plentifully rewardeth the proud doer."
Psalm 31:19,23

Finally, we need to emphatically state that we enter into

worship because God wants us to and because He alone is worthy of it!

> *"But the hour cometh, and now is, when the true worshippers shall worship the Father in spirit and in truth; for the Father seeketh such to worship Him."*
>
> John 4:23

Notice that God seeks a people to worship Him. This has been the case throughout history. God's people are called to be a people of worship. The world will know them as worshippers of the Living God.

> *"The four and twenty elders fall down before Him that lives forever and ever and cast their crowns before the throne, saying,*
>
> *Thou art worthy, O Lord, to receive glory and honor and power; for Thou hast created all things, and for Thy pleasure they are and were created."*
>
> Revelation 4:10-11

God is worthy! How much we need to emphasize that in our worship. He is worthy of far more than we can ever give. He is infinitely more worthy than what He usually receives from Christians in worship! Notice in the preceding Scripture that all things are and were created for His pleasure. It is a fact beyond human comprehension that the Creator of the universe, the Living God, actually desires fellowship with us. Can we ever grasp just how intense is God's love for us? Can we fathom the depth of fellowship and communion He desires to share with us? As we reflect on the fact that God sent His Son to die in order that our fellowship with Him might be restored and that, through Jesus, we might be adopted into the family of God, we should overflow with praise and adoration! Can we ever do anything to repay God or earn His favor? Never! He lovingly asks us to accept the truth of Jesus' death and resurrection and then to worship Him . . . to share in His love . . . to bear witness to His glory.

"O Lord, our Lord, how excellent is Thy name in all the earth, who hast set Thy glory above the heavens!

When I consider Thy heavens, the work of Thy fingers, the moon and the stars, which Thou hast ordained,

What is man, that Thou are mindful of him? And the son of man, that Thou visitest him?

O Lord, our Lord, how excellent is Thy name in all the earth."

Psalm 8:1,3,4,9

Teach us, O Lord, to become worshippers. Prepare our hearts so that we may boldly and joyfully enter your presence. May our lives proclaim Your grace and holiness.

"Wherefore, receiving a kingdom which cannot be moved, let us have grace, by which we may serve God acceptably with reverence and godly fear;

For our God is a consuming fire."

Hebrews 12:28-29

"This people have I formed for Myself; they shall show forth My praise."

Isaiah 43:21

Our response? Amen and Hallelujah!

Chapter 5

BECOMING A WORSHIPER

"The Lord does not look at the things man looks at. Man looks at the outward appearance, but the Lord looks at the heart."   1 Samuel 16:7(**NIV**)

Each of us is given gifts and abilities which contribute to the strengthening and ministry of the Body of Christ. Some are gifted teachers, others have God given ability in leading people to Christ, still others may utilize administrative abilities, and so it goes. There is, however, one remarkable fact that we need to grasp. Absolutely every one of us has a Divine calling to be a worshipper! As mentioned earlier, worship is the most essential aspect of our Christian lives. It is the source of our strength, the ultimate object of all activity and ministry, and the beginning and end of our journey with Christ. Where then do we start? How do we become worshippers? The answer lies in the heart and in the attitudes which emerge from the condition of our heart. God examines our hearts carefully and desires to bless those individuals who set their hearts in line with Him. For example:

> "For the eyes of the Lord run to and fro throughout the whole earth, to show Himself strong in the behalf of them whose heart is perfect toward Him."
>
> 2 Chronicles 16:9

Therefore, on our pilgrimage toward the summit called "worship in spirit and truth", let us prepare our hearts for the journey.

> "Examine me, O Lord, and prove me; test my heart and my mind."
>
> Psalm 26:2

BROKENNESS

Brokenness is the beginning. I do not wish to sound overly "spiritual" or "mystical" because I believe that God is very practical in His dealings with us. However, at some point in our lives we must run into the Cross. For some it is a head on collision. For others, the road on which they have been traveling merely comes to an end. The Cross is that area in our lives where God's will intersects with our will. We encounter Jesus in a life changing way and something inside of us breaks. For some, real brokenness occurs when they discover Christ as Savior. For others, brokenness occurs when they gain a full and even dramatic revelation of Christ as Lord. Tragically for some it never really occurs.

When we are broken, we no longer seek to do Christ's work in the "glorious" power of our own strength and abilities. We no longer, for example, expect to redeem the world with gifted planning and energetic programming. How much of our Christian work is carried on in a spirit of "strong human ability." How often we get so carried away with doing God's work "for Him" that we never even stop to ask, "Lord, are You still here?" How terrible it is when worship is undertaken in this spirit! It very often is. Only when we come to the end of the road of "accomplishment through our personal strength and zeal" do we realize how unclean our garments really are. At this point a feeling of being tainted and worthless descends. "O Lord, there is no good work in me. Only You are holy!" It is by the grace of God that we are able to come to this place.

How very blessed we are when we can thoroughly cast off our personal goals and ambitions which have become gift wrapped in "spiritual paper" and be content to sit at Jesus' feet and listen to what He has to teach us. Our only motive then is learning to love Him more fully. Obedience begins here.

Frequently, what we do in the Lord's name is subconsciously undertaken to bring us glory. "Only You, Lord, are worthy to receive glory and honor and praise now and forever!" Out of the seeming wreckage of a broken and contrite spirit, God begins to create a beautiful, tender plant. This plant is one which receives nourishment directly from its Creator and which, as it grows, reflects more and more of its Maker's glorious handiwork. Consider the following scriptures.

> "The Lord is near unto those who are of a broken heart, and saves such as be of a contrite spirit." *Psalm 34:18*

> "The sacrifices of God are a broken spirit; a broken and contrite heart, O God, Thou wilt not despise." *Psalm 51:17*

And finally, in the words of Jesus:

> "Blessed are the poor in spirit; for theirs is the kingdom of heaven." *Matthew 5:3*

At this point it is crucial that we be completely honest with ourselves and with God. What are our motives? Have we come to the place where we can say, "Thy will be done!" at all costs? If we are able to say yes to that question, we will begin to experience true rest and peace. It is extremely difficult to enter into meaningful and acceptable worship if we are driven by a striving spirit. Whenever I think of brokenness, I usually find myself reflecting on the story in the 7th chapter of Luke's Gospel.

"And, behold, a woman in the city, who was a sinner, when she knew that Jesus was eating in the Pharisee's house, brought an alabaster box of ointment,

And stood at His feet behind Him, weeping; and began to wash His feet with tears, and did wipe them with the hair of her head, and kissed His feet, and anointed them with the ointment."

Luke 7:37-38

Not only did Jesus forgive this woman's sins, He commented on her faith!

"And He said to the woman, 'Thy faith hath saved thee; go in peace.'"　　　*Luke 7:50*

Worship arises in purity and beauty out of a broken spirit.

More of us, like the patriarch Jacob, need to "walk with a limp." (Genesis 32:31) Jacob symbolized profound human cunning and craftiness. Through scheming and planning he obtained what he wanted. At Peniel he had reached the end of his road. He was going back to meet with Esau, and he really did not know whether Esau would kill him or receive him. His cunning could not help him here. It was at this very point, like so many of us, that he wrestled with the Lord. So great was his strength that the turmoil lasted all night! Finally, the Lord touched him and he was changed. From then on he walked with a "limp."

I have met many Christians who were "on fire for God." Some of them get quite frustrated trying to make God's plans fit into their zeal. Others leave a trail of spiritual wreckage, even though they sincerely believed their actions to be grounded in God's word and thereby in His will. When we take this zealous heart and bring it to the altar of brokenness, we then have the real makings of a servant of the Lord. Only after experiencing brokenness can we be clay, able to be molded by the Master Potter into a vessel of His choosing.

It is always hard to lay down dreams and ambitions held for years. I experienced this several years ago. From the age of 5 I received rigorous musical training. Music became the passion of my life. It had become my idol. After becoming a Christian, I did what so many of us do, and simply moved my secular goals and ambitions over to the Christian arena. Of course, they looked splendid with a nice religious coating spread on them. God is merciful. By His grace I ran into a continuous stream of problems and closed doors. How clearly the day it ended remains in my mind. I was driving to work and reflecting on the many frustrations I had experienced when I said, "Lord, I don't understand it and it doesn't make sense. I have trained in music all of my life, but it just isn't working. Every time I have tried to use my abilities in Your service something has been definitely wrong. I give it up. If it is Your will, music will be for me a thing of the past. Please, Lord, help me to do only those things in my life that bring glory to Your name."

At that moment, by an act of my will, my ambitions died. I strangely felt an inner peace and as though somehow I had been cleansed. As it turned out, from that time on God has gently and lovingly restored the gift of music to my life. However, it is His choice and my devotion to Him would be no different even if it had not been. I sincerely feel that, even now, I could willingly walk away from it if the Lord so directed. Still, my daily prayer is that anything I do in life will bring glory to God and to Him alone. "Lord, make me an instrument of Your praise!"

> *"He that finds his life shall lose it, and he that loses his life for My sake shall find it."*
> *Matthew 10:39*

> *"Then said Jesus unto His disciples, If any man will come after Me, let him deny himself, and take up his cross, and follow Me.*
> *For whosoever will save his life shall lose it, and whosoever will lose his life for My sake shall find it."*
> *Matthew 16:24-25*

Finally, a broken spirit allows us to worship freely with our brothers and sisters in Christ. In his book entitled, "The Release Of The Spirit"[1] Watchman Nee refers to us as vessels filled with a precious perfume. It is only when the vessels are broken that the perfumes can flow together and fill the air with Divine fragrance. What a vivid picture that is. Most of the time we keep "our perfume" completely bottled up in rigidly sealed containers. The sound that we then hear (which is usually called "worship") is the clanking of sealed bottles knocking together. Brokenness is beautiful. It allows God to shape us so that His love can flow freely through us to others. We must remember, however, that no matter how

[2]Watchman Nee, *The Release Of The Spirit,* (Sure Foundation Publishers, Copyright 1965.)

mature we feel or how greatly the Lord has used us, we must continually go back to our own "Peniels." Worship is a way of life. Brokenness allows worship to flow. We never grow out of a humble, broken spirit. We must continually go back to these waters for cleansing in order to be of real use to God and to allow His light to shine brilliantly in and through us.

"Who is like unto the Lord, our God, Who dwells on high,

Who humbles Himself to behold the things that are in heaven, and in the earth!"

Psalm 113:5-6

SERVANTHOOD

"Let this mind be in you, which was also in Christ Jesus,

Who, being in the form of God, thought it not robbery to be equal with God,

But made Himself of no reputation, and took upon Him the form of a servant, and was made in the likeness of men;

And, being found in fashion as a man, He humbled Himself and became obedient unto death, even the death of the cross.

Wherefore, God also has highly exalted Him, and given a name which is above every name,

That at the name of Jesus every knee should bow, of things in heaven, and things in earth, and things under the earth,

And that every tongue should confess that Jesus Christ is Lord, to the glory of God, the Father." Philippians 2:5-11

Out of a broken, humble spirit emerges a spirit of servanthood. This spirit prepares our hearts for worship. Have you ever tried to worship in a gathering where there seemed to be a strong feeling of self-righteousness, pride, and egocentricity? In such meetings there is not much room for God (or for you). In this type of setting we frequently have lots of "form" but little genuine spirit. Oh, there may be a degree of fellowship, but it usually is rather plastic and shallow. I question whether or not God is actually present when we worship out of tacet homage to our own egos.

Contrast this type of worship with the experience of going before God in humility and brokenness, wanting nothing more than to give all that is in us to Him and to others. A servant spirit seeks to do just that. It desires to give more than to receive. As is customary with our gracious Lord, the more we earnestly desire to give to Him and others, the more He sheds His love abroad in our hearts.

"I therefore, the prisoner of the Lord, beseech you that you walk worthy of the vocation to which you are called,

With all lowliness and meekness, with long-

suffering, forbearing one another in love,

Endeavoring to keep the unity of the Spirit in the bond of peace."   Ephesians 4:1-3

To be a servant means that we make sacrifices out of our love for God in order that others may succeed. It means that we lay down "self" in order to help others stand. It means that we reach out to those who lack understanding, not just to fellowship in their dim light, but lovingly give ourselves to encourage them to stand up and walk. It is a spirit that says, "How wonderful the Lord is! Won't you share with me in worshipping Him?" The spirit of a servant is not one that compromises the truth. It does not yield endlessly to those who make demands merely to placate them. Rather, it is a spirit that "speaks the truth in love." (Ephesians 4:15) It is a spirit that walks humbly in heart and mind and yet reaches out sacrificially to those who need, want, hunger, and thirst. Servanthood makes real our spirit of brokenness. The marvelous light that God implants in a broken vessel begins to shine brightly as that vessel, in Christ's love, begins to serve others.

"And be kind one to another, tenderhearted, forgiving one another, even as God, for Christ's sake, has forgiven you.

Be, therefore, followers of God, as dear children;

And walk in love, as Christ also has loved us, and has given Himself for us an offering and a sacrifice to God for a sweet-smelling savor."

Ephesians 4:32-5:2

Can we really rejoice in the success of another? Are we able to sacrifice precious dreams, effort, and time to enable others to make it? Are we willing to do it even if we know that no one but God will know and appreciate the cost we have borne? Can we serve others knowing that we probably won't even receive a small "Thank you?" To be a humble, obedient servant is to know and exercise God's transforming love. Listen to the Apostle John.

"Beloved, if God so loved us, we ought also to love one another.

No man has seen God at any time. If we love one another, God dwells in us and His love is perfected in us."

1 John 4:11-12

And,

"He that loves his brother abides in the light, and there is no occasion of stumbling in him."

1 John 2:10

The heart of a servant allows us to experience God and to bring others into His fullness. A gathering of broken, humble, serving spirits united in worship of God is a glorious experience. In this setting we truly "abide in His light." Our lives reflect it.

*"In the light of the King's countenance is life,
and His favor is like a cloud of the latter rain."*
Proverbs 16:15

PATIENCE

*"I wait for the Lord, my soul doth wait, and
in His word do I hope.
My soul waiteth for the Lord more than
they that watch for the morning; I say, more than
they that watch for the morning."*
Psalm 130:5-6

I must confess that, for me, this is really a tough one.
Patience is something that I constantly need to work on.
Actually, God has been teaching me quite a bit on this
subject. It is amazing how those little things that bring out the
impatient spirit in us keep surfacing until we have a radical
dealing with the root problem. Sometimes I feel like the little
boy who is running furiously down the hall and whose father
suddenly picks him up by the shirt collar. If you have ever
seen that humorous picture, you will notice that the little
boy's legs keep on going for quite a while until it dawns on
him that his feet are not touching the ground and he is going
nowhere. Patience of spirit is essential to becoming a
worshipper. We cannot sit at the Lord's feet, wait on Him,
and spend considerable time worshipping Him if we are
agitated by or driven by a restless, impatient spirit. I
remember how I used to sit down to worship and pray and
would start by saying something like, "Lord, You are great

and wonderful. It is good to praise You." Then my mind would immediately say, "OK Lord, now that I've said that, what's next?" In our society we are always in a terrific hurry to get somewhere. "Where are you going in such a hurry?" "I don't know, but if I don't get going I'll be late!" The thought of sitting quietly at God's feet and worshiping Him without conscious reference to the clock is quite foreign to us.

I must here confess to having a very bad attitude towards those digital watches that go "Beep, beep" on the hour. In church, how often I have been in prayer only to hear a piercing "Beep, beep" come knifing into my ears as an additional reminder that we are hopelessly chained to a pace dictated by the clock. (I also have a problem with cuckoo clocks. Have you ever been in a home prayer meeting when one of those things goes off?! Or how about those clocks that sound like "Big Ben" every hour? Help! I am quite aware that the Lord will mercifully lead me through an endless array of clangs, bangs, dings, and dongs until not even clocks deter my worship of him!)

We need to free ourselves of restricting worship totally by the boundaries of time. This, however, is absolutely not a case for an insensitivity or legalistic attitude towards time. I have endured worship services and meetings that ran on for hours and hours in order to prove a presence of "spirituality." (There is somewhat of a limit to how long any person can sit! To say nothing about subjecting children to the "everlasting Gospel!") To tightly and rigidly program worship down to the second is error. To run on endlessly in order to prove "how much we love the Lord" is also not right. Let us be flexible so that the Holy Spirit can move in our midst and let us free ourselves of the demanding fetters of the clock.

"Be still, and know that I am God; . . ."

Psalm 46:10

To be patient means that we have ceased striving and busyness. It means that we possess a calm expectancy concerning God's working in our lives. We know inwardly that God is in control. We learn to wait on the Lord, to be sensitive to the still small voice of the Spirit, and to receive what God has for us gladly, openly, and freely. We can reason and argue with God for quite some time, but He just does not seem to be committed to our well-planned agendas.

Patience also allows us to fellowship with those individuals who are difficult to love. It therefore supports our spirit of servanthood. We are giving people time to grow. We are not force feeding them. However, we additionally are not allowing the truth to be submerged and ourselves to be taken advantage of by those whose real agenda says "NO" to growth. Patience, in the context of our relationships to others, is closely related to longsuffering. We view our brothers and sisters in Christ as persons of infinite worth, created by God. We suffer and grieve when they go astray, and like the father with the prodigal son, we wait with patient, loving, and helpful arms when they come back. We share in their trials and problems while recognizing God's eternal hand on their lives.

God is eternal. Eternity is forever. When we worship, we step into the eternal. We fellowship with the God Who was, Who is, and Who is to come. May God teach us not to inhibit His presence with a restless, hurried, and impatient spirit. Rather, let us rest in the Lord in whom we live and move and have our being. We may have developed such modern day wonders as instant coffee, instant mashed potatoes, (and just about instant everything,) but let us never expect "instant worship." God is patient with us. I am eternally grateful for that, aren't you?

TEACHABLE SPIRIT

"For as he thinks in his heart, so is he . . ."
Proverbs 23:7

If we are to learn of God and experience more and more of His fullness, we must develop a teachable spirit. In our modern world, knowledge abounds and we are flooded with experts, whatever the field. People used to claim that we would have a better world if only we could educate people. What a blind alley that has turned out to be! In the first place, knowledge apart from humble submission to God breeds arrogance and ultimately error.

In Christianity, we have been led to believe that this or that particular study would bring "maturity." We have tended to clutch onto quick answers to life's problems arising out of someone's sudden "revelation." While there may be truth in many things God is revealing and renewing in His word, there are no shortcuts to the path of life with God. Knowledge of God's word is essential. However, we need to remember that the Christian life is a journey, a pilgrimage to the heavenly city. It is not a matter of arrival. I have encountered some Christians who were totally unteachable because they sincerely felt that they had "arrived."

Sometimes an unteachable spirit emerges from extensive "Bible knowledge." People like this can quote countless

Scriptures, and they also can "beat you over the head with them." Once again, knowledge does not mean maturity. Knowledge also does not automatically impart sensitivity to the Holy Spirit. I have run into some clergy who felt that they needed to learn nothing about worship. (What can you possibly teach anyone who "knows it all?") By the grace of God I hope to keep on learning!

Sometimes people are unteachable because of fear of venturing into new territory. There can be fear in having to walk in faith, depending solely on God for provision and sustenance. Oh, but this walk is where life really takes on meaning! Sometimes we must leave the padded security of what is traditionally known and practiced in order to see God's light for today. Never do we depart from God's word; but, if we allow Him, God reveals more and more about ourselves, Himself, and His will for us.

In order to become a worshipper, we need a real openness to the voice of the Lord. We must learn to listen. (A lost art!) In order to hear clearly we need freedom from the bondage of mental preconception anchored in man's tradition and not necessarily affirmed in God's word.

Finally, pride and arrogance prohibit a teachable spirit. The Lord seeks hungry disciples, not knowledgeable pharisees. Recently, I was attending the state convention of my denomination and was one of many speaking on several key issues in a workshop. Shortly after the discussion began, a man took the floor and gave a classic demonstration of the haughty, arrogant spirit. He began by citing his long membership in a very prestigious (and well to do) church. Next, he informed everyone that he was a state representative and therefore possessed genuine expertise on all of the issues. To say that he was unteachable would be an understatement.

There was not the slightest opening in his mind for any new light. He absolutely knew it all and felt his mission was to enlighten and correct anyone who might disagree with him. It was as though he were saying, "God is all-knowing and wise, therefore, I am convinced that He agrees with me!"

All of us must examine our attitudes to make certain that we are teachable. A humble, teachable spirit opens the door to receiving God's truth and paves the way for meaningful communication and fellowship. We will serve God much more effectively and be far greater stewards of time and responsibility if we will commit ourselves to spending quality time before the many church committee and board meetings worshipping God and praying for open, humble, and teachable spirits! How marvelously that would pave the way for real unity.

Lord, we sincerely want You to teach us Your ways. Teach us Your will. Give us eyes to see and ears to hear. Create, O Lord, a right spirit within us. Reveal to us anything that stands in the way of understanding Your truth.

"The heart of him that has understanding seeks knowledge,"   Proverbs 15:14

HUNGER AND THIRST

"Ho, everyone that thirsts, come to the waters, . . ."   Isaiah 55:1

Do we really desire to know God? How great is our thirst for His presence? How deep is our hunger for true worship?

These are pivotal questions that underlie spiritual growth. A worshipper hungers for God!

"As the hart pants after the water brooks, so pants my soul after Thee, O God.
My soul thirsts for God, for the living God; when shall I come and appear before God?"
Psalm 42:1-2

I know of no greater curse than to lose our hunger for God. How many Christians have lost their zeal? How often do we see churches pillaged by complacency, apathy, and compromise? The "concerns of the world" will, if allowed, extinguish the fire that burns within us. Lack of personal dedication and time spent with the Lord, busyness, laziness, and overcommitment to things which draw us away from God all lend their destructive touch to worship. What generally happens to a group of Christians who lose their "fire" is a diminishing of personal and corporate vision, a loss of the unique sense of being called out of the world to be God's people, and a real loss in power in worship and ministry.

When this happens we try to keep some sort of religious momentum going by skillful programming, endless activities and programs, and by adopting regular "workable routines" in worship. As a symptom of our coldness, we develop an abrasive harshness to anyone who suggests in any way that we have gotten off the track. "How dare you suggest that this fine group of church members is lacking!"

Unfortunately, when complacency creeps into our spiritual lives, we see two types of fruit emerge. We either see a falling away or the development of an intense self-righteousness. Even worse, we begin to go back to the law. Our Christian standing is then not measured honestly by our heart relationship to God, but is justified by our attendance at worship services, Bible studies, men's and women's church functions and fellowship groups, pancake suppers, and rummage sales! The point here is that all activities undertaken in Christ's name and directed by the Holy Spirit can bring blessing if our hearts are in the right place. If we are doing it because it is something "we are supposed to do," then we have a deeper problem.

I vividly remember one particular incident in my own life. I was new to the Christian faith and was bursting with zeal. At the time, my family belonged to a large church and the pastor asked me to be on a committee to draft a statement of mission for the church. (How often this noble task results in religious verbiage!) In any event, many key church members attended the meeting. A lengthy list of quite worthy goals was established. (Spreading the Gospel, providing help for the needy, hope for the hopeless, being a lighthouse for the world, etc.)

Then, I really did it! Innocently, I asked, "Are we really doing these things? Are we the people in God's eyes that we think we are?" Suddenly there was profound silence. As I glanced around I was met with more than a few angry stares. "Are you implying that this isn't God's church?" "Let me tell you, young man, I've been a member here for 20 years and there are lots of fine people here!" "What are you implying, anyway?" What's wrong with our church?" "The idea of raising those kinds of questions to men and women who give so much of their time!" And so it went. I plunged headlong into a lions' den, but really learned something that night. If you are bold enough (or naive enough) to question the status quo of a smoothly functioning religious organization, be prepared, like Elijah, to make a fervent dash for the hills!

"The Lord looked down from heaven upon the children of men, to see if there were any that did understand and seek God."   Psalm 14:2

Where there is genuine spiritual hunger, there exists a chance for God to break through in a sovereign way. There is hope and expectation. When people truly seeking God come together to worship, a Divine sense of intensity prevails. Things get exciting! May the words spoken in the pulpits across this land ignite a hunger for God! How earnestly I pray that the words in this book kindle a fire in you to seek God passionately and with your whole heart. What a magnificent blessing it is to enter God's presence and feel our hearts burning for more of Him. When Peter recognized the resurrected Jesus from his fishing boat, he "did cast himself into the sea." (John 21) He could not even wait for the boat to reach shore. That is zeal for the Lord!

"And they said one to another, Did not our heart burn within us, while He talked with us along the way, and while He opened to us the scriptures."   Luke 24:32

Being with the Lord not only opens our eyes to His truth, it sets our hearts ablaze! Remember this. God honors those who seek.

"If thou seek Him, He will be found by thee . . ."   1 Chronicles 28:9

Like so many things in our Christian faith, seeking God requires a decision. Being a worshipper requires making a decision. We must decide to seek God with our whole hearts, souls, minds, and bodies, and to adore and glorify Him.

Finally, may we fully realize that fellowship with God, worshiping our Lord and Maker, is an end in itself. Indeed, it is our ultimate end. It is a goal worth seeking at any cost!

"Oh, come, let us worship and bow down; let us kneel before the Lord our Maker."
Psalm 95:6

May we shout a hearty "Amen" to the prayer of David.

"One thing have I desired of the Lord, that will I seek after: that I may dwell in the house of the Lord all the days of my life, to behold the beauty of the Lord, and to inquire in His temple."
Psalm 27:4

PASSION AND INTENSITY

These two words have crept into many of the pages of this book. Our western society has been described as being "cooly rational." We are a people who guard feelings and try not to "expose" our emotions . . . except, at sporting events. How strange it is that we cherish "intensity" in participating or viewing sports, but try to keep the exercise of our faith in a very controlled box. As mentioned earlier, we often describe worship with adjectives like "decent, lovely, nice, reverent, orderly, or controlled." The Israelites worshipped God with intensity and passion whenever they walked with Him. Should not intenstiy and passion describe the condition of our hearts toward God?

> *"Love the Lord your God with all your heart and with all your soul and with all your strength."* Deuteronomy 6:5(NIV)

These words spoken by Moses and affirmed by Jesus show passionate, intense devotion to God. We need to seek God with a heart set on Him, not one divided with cravings for other things.

> *"Teach me your way, O Lord; I will walk in your truth; unite my heart to fear your name."* Psalm 86:11

To become a worshipper we cease trying to fit God into a narrow compartment of our lives. He is Lord of the entirety of our lives. We do not allow compromise to dampen our fire. A heart full of passion for the Lord is not a heart ruled by emotion. It is a heart firmly rooted in the purposes of God. It is a heart that states with the deepest level of conviction, "But as for me and my house, we will serve the Lord." (Joshua 24:15)

THE FEAR OF THE LORD

"Behold, the eye of the Lord is upon those who fear Him, upon those who hope in His mercy,"
                                        Psalm 33:18

The fear of the Lord is a theme that runs throughout Scripture. Indeed, the destiny of men and nations rests on this concept. The fear of the Lord is positive. It does not refer to a negative, oppressive fear of a tyrannical god. Rather, it is a holy, reverent, wondrous awe of a God whose majesty, splendor, and power exceed our comprehension. The fear of the Lord is a mark of God's people.

"And I will make an everlasting covenant with them, that I will not turn away from doing them good, but I will put My fear in their hearts, that they shall not depart from Me."
                                        Jeremiah 32:40

"Thou hast given a banner to them that fear Thee, that it may be displayed because of the truth."
                                        Psalm 60:4

The Scriptures on this subject are plentiful. This reflects just how important it is. A worshipper knows the fear of the Lord. It is a condition of heart and mind that allows wisdom, knowledge, and growth in the Lord to occur. Consider these Scriptures.

"The fear of the Lord is the beginning of knowl-edge, . . ." Proverbs 1:7

"The fear of the Lord is the beginning of wisdom, and the knowledge of the Holy One is understanding." Proverbs 9:10

"The fear of the Lord is a fountain of life, to depart from the snares of death." Proverbs 14:27

And finally,

"The fear of the Lord is clean, enduring forever; . . ." Psalm 19:9

A "heart perfect toward God" is a heart that knows and understands the fear of the Lord. That is a teachable heart.

"What man is he that fears the Lord? Him shall He teach in the way that He shall choose. The secret of the Lord is with those who fear Him, and He will show them His covenant." Psalm 25:12,14

The fear of the Lord is also present at the culmination of history.

"Who shall not fear Thee, O Lord, and glorify

Thy name? For Thou only art Holy; for all nations shall come and worship before Thee;"

Revelation 15:4

A worshipper bows before the power and majesty of God. He acknowledges God's magnificent glory and he is broken at the revelation of God's boundless love. Let us press on, with the fear of the Lord in our innermost being, to become a people bearing testimony to His glory and grace.

"But as for me, I will come into Thy house in the multitude of Thy mercy; and in Thy fear will I worship toward Thy holy temple."

Psalm 5:7

"He will bless those who fear the Lord, both small and great."   *Psalm 115:13*

HOLINESS

"Having, therefore, these promises, dearly beloved, let us cleanse ourselves from all filthiness of the flesh and spirit, perfecting holiness in the fear of God."   *2 Corinthians 7:1*

Earlier we discussed the fact that God is holy and that worship reflects that fact. As we draw close to Him, we are made painfully aware of our uncleanness and unrighteousness.

To be a worshipper, the concept of holiness needs to become a reality, even a "burden," in our lives. Holiness is not a call to some sort of legalistic bondage where our behavior is determined by a complex set of rules. Our righteousness is in Christ and no other. It is certainly not in written or unwritten rules.

Holiness is a door to liberty through sanctification in God's will. It means that our hearts are set apart unto God. By Christ's death on the cross we are reconciled to God. By His shed blood, we are cleansed. Our holiness is established in Christ. The working of God's grace, applying the righteousness of Jesus in our hearts and lives and being cleansed from domination of the "carnal man" is to be worked out daily. We must remember that without hearts of holiness, we cannot come fully into God's presence.

"Who shall ascend into the hill of the Lord?
Or who shall stand in His holy place?
He who has clean hands, and a pure heart, who has not lifted up his soul unto vanity, nor sworn deceitfully."　　　　　*Psalm 24:3-4*

Several years ago a lady in our prayer group made an interesting observation. She said, "You know, it doesn't seem like the new Christian songs are ever about the Cross or the Blood of Jesus." I thought for a while and then I had to agree. I could think of very few. In fact, how many new songs deal with the area of holiness? It has been my observation that the first major step in falling away from the Christian faith is a lack of concern about or an outright cynicism with regard to holiness. The liberty we have in Christ quickly leads to licentiousness when divorced from a heart dedicated to personal holiness before a sovereign and holy God. In the words of the Apostle Peter:

"But, as He who has called you is holy, so be ye holy in all manner of life,

Because it is written, Be ye holy; for I am holy."

1 Peter 1:15-16

Have you ever worshipped God and been deeply moved by a revelation on His holiness? Furthermore, have you ever had that experience and then, shortly thereafter, been in the presence of someone who was harsh, insensitive, or perhaps even crude? What a painful experience! God's holiness is awesome. It makes us want to bow down and shield ourselves.

Again, we remember that Jesus, the Holy One of Israel (Isaiah 43:3), cleanses us through His blood. (Hebrews 13:12) Let our hearts by faith continually renew our cleansing. Let our minds be refreshed and purified by immersion in Scripture. Holiness is our Divine calling. It is God's requirement. We must worship God in holiness. Praise God for giving us the means and the provision!

"And a highway shall be there, and a way, and it shall be called The way of holiness; . . ."

Isaiah 35:8

"you also, like living stones, are being built into a spiritual house to be a holy priesthood, offering spiritual sacrifices acceptable to God through Jesus Christ"

1 Peter 2:5(NIV)

"For God has not called us unto uncleanness, but unto holiness." 1 Thessalonians 4:7

And, let us soberly reflect on God's solemn warning to the end of the age.

"He that is unjust, let him be unjust still; and he that is filthy, let him be filthy still; and he that is righteous, let him be righteous still, and he that is holy, let him be holy still."

Revelation 22:11

The choice is ours.

THANKFULNESS

"Enter into His gates with thanksgiving, and into His courts with praise; be thankful unto Him, and bless His name." Psalm 100:4

A thankful heart is one that responds to the awareness of God's sovereign grace in our lives. A heart abounding with thanksgiving is one prepared to offer praise to God. We need to spend some time reflecting on what God has done in our lives. We usually take thanksgiving far too lightly. When Jesus healed the ten lepers, only one returned glorifying God

74

and giving thanks. Jesus asked, "Where are the other nine?" (Luke 17) Being thankful is more than mere "lip service." It is more than a mealtime grace or a brief prayer of thanksgiving read on Sunday morning. The spirit of being thankful needs to reach deep down into our souls. Reflect for a moment on the outcome of those who are not thankful, specifically those who grumble and murmer.

"Neither murmer ye, as some of them also murmered, and were destroyed by the destroyer."
1 Corinthians 10:10

Some suggest that it is a helpful exercise to list all of the things we have to be thankful about. For me, thinking about being a member of God's very own family does it. God is so very practical. Consider briefly the difference you feel in spending time with someone who is tremendously grateful about something and full of thanksgiving as compared with someone who is bitter, resentful, and grumbling. Is it any wonder God chooses to fellowship with those individuals who have thanksgiving in their hearts?

One recent specific example of thanksgiving comes to mind. Our place of business is located near a river. A short while back, that river flooded terribly and it looked as though we would undergo heavy losses. My father and I hiked into the plant early one Sunday morning to try and salvage a few things before the waters came. It looked bad. Much to our delight, the waters stopped rising a little over 100 yards from our plant. That evening the entire family had dinner at a local restaurant. Much to our surprise, my father suddenly stood up and lead everyone (in the whole room!) in a prayer of thanksgiving. When you are really thankful, you want others to know it!

God commands us to be thankful.

". . . be ye thankful."　　　　　　　*Colossians 3:15*

It is for our own good. Think of the medical bills that would be avoided if we concentrated our thoughts on things for which we should be thankful instead of on problems and tragedies. In this regard, I have freed myself from addiction to the network news. I still find out what is going on in the world but what incredible peace has resulted from freeing myself from the daily bombardment of bad news and "editorial comment." (Really, God is in control and more good things are happening than we are led to believe.) We must guard our minds from the dark negativism and gloomy feeling of impending doom fostered by the secular minds.

"Be anxious for nothing, but in everything, by prayer and supplication with thanksgiving, let your requests be made known unto God.

And the peace of God, which passeth all understanding, shall keep your hearts and minds through Christ Jesus.

Finally, brethren, whatever things are true, whatever things are honest, whatever things are pure, whatever things are of good report; if there be any virtue, and if there by any praise, think on these things."　　　　　　*Philippians 4:6-8*

What a promise! We do have our part. I heartily recommend the above Scripture to start your morning instead of your favorite newscast!

It is God's definite will for us to be thankful.

"In everything give thanks; for this is the will of God in Christ Jesus concerning you."

1 Thessalonians 5:18

It is very significant that the next verse after the above Scripture says, "Quench not the Spirit." A heart that is not thankful certainly does quench the Spirit! Reflect once more on the implications of being thankful as opposed to being discontented in relation to faith, fellowship, prayer, and praise. We really cannot function at all in the spiritual realm without thanksgiving, can we? It is not just something God prefers, it is absolutely essential. I know that there are times when it is extremely difficult to feel thankful. Nevertheless, God honors our obedience in "entering His gates with thanksgiving." In fact, I think it means more to Him when it is difficult for us. At those times we make a decision of our will not to let circumstances rob us of our fellowship with God. We insist on being thankful. God knows exactly how difficult it is. He is there with us! A worshipper comes before God filled with thanksgiving. What other posture can we possibly have when we realize that our God, so great . . . so magnificent . . . so holy . . . so powerful, loves us . . . sacrificially!

"After this I beheld and, lo, a great multitude, which no man could number, of all

nations, and kindreds, and peoples, and tongues, stood before the Lamb, clothed with white robes, and palms in their hands.

And cried with a loud voice, saying, Salvation to our God who sitteth upon the throne, and unto the Lamb.

And all the angels stood round about the throne, and about the elders and the four living creatures, and fell before the throne on their faces, and worshipped God,

Saying, Amen! Blessing, and glory, and wisdom, and thanksgiving, and honor, and power, and might be unto our God forever and ever. Amen."   *Revelation 7:9-12*

JOY

"Therefore, the redeemed of the Lord shall return, and come with singing unto Zion, and everlasting joy shall be upon their head; they shall obtain gladness and joy, and sorrow and mourning shall flee away."   *Isaiah 51:11*

A heart bursting with thanksgiving gives rise to the release of joy. Joy is quite a subject. It is so essential to our well-being and yet, it is so often misunderstood. Originally, I had planned to call a chapter in this book, "The Problem With Joy!" Frequently our worship services allow no room for genuine expressions of joy, to say nothing of spontaneous expressions of joy! Also, place a grumbler or a murmurer in worship next to a person captivated with exhuberant joy and you have a volatile mix.

Joy is a privilege of worship. It is one of the real fruits of the Christian life. It has been said that the entire message of the Gospel can be summed up in one word, "Rejoice!" Rejoice, our Savior is born! Rejoice, our Savior is risen! Rejoice, our Savior reigns over all principalities and powers! How we need to know and express the depths of joy that are ours in Jesus.

> "Therefore, with joy shall ye draw water out of the wells of salvation."　　Isaiah 12:3

It is joy of the Lord that sustains us and fills our lives with fruitful hope.

> "The joy of the Lord is your strength."　　Nehemiah 8:10

We have seen so many pictures of a suffering Jesus. Do we realize that His ministry was one of joy?

> "The Spirit of the Lord God is upon me, because the Lord has anointed me to preach good tidings unto the meek; He has sent me to bind up the brokenhearted, to proclaim liberty to the captives, and the opening of the prison to those who

79

are bound;

To proclaim the acceptable year of the Lord, and the day of vengeance of our God; to comfort all that mourn;

To appoint unto those who mourn in Zion, to give unto them beauty for ashes, the oil of joy for mourning, the garment of praise for the spirit of heaviness, that they might be called trees of righteousness, the planting of the Lord, that He might be glorified."   Isaiah 61:1-3

There is no limit to the number of books that could be written on that passage alone. Notice the phrase, "the oil of joy." Consider the angelic proclamation of Jesus' birth.

"And the angel said unto them, Fear not; for, behold, I bring you good tidings of great joy, which shall be to all people."   Luke 2:10

Jesus wanted us to experience joy. What a blessed ministry His was.

"These things have I spoken unto you, that My joy might remain in you, and that your joy might be full."   John 15:11

". . . ask, and you shall receive, that your joy may be full."   John 16:24

> *"And now come I to you; and these things I speak in the world, that they might have My joy fulfilled in themselves."* John 17:13

Not only is heaven a place of joy, but the hosts of heaven rejoice over us when we become members through Christ of God's family. What a fantastic thought.!

> *"Likewise, I say unto you, there is joy in the presence of the angels of God over one sinner that repents."* Luke 15:10

Oh, what a blessing it is to come into God's presence in joy, to share His joy, to experience and share in the fulness of joy flowing from the hearts of others. Where there is joy, there is hope and strength. Where there is joy, God's peace reigns! Is it not tragic that genuine joy of the Lord is so often absent from worship? To the Church, let us pray the words of David.

> *"Restore unto me the joy of Thy salvation, . . .* Psalm 51:12

As we come together to give ourselves in worship of God, let us joyfully ponder His grace . . . our destiny.

> *"And the ransomed of the Lord shall return, and come to Zion with songs and everlasting joy upon their heads; they shall obtain joy and gladness, and sorrow and sighing shall flee away."* Isaiah 35:10

What a glorious calling we have. What magnificent treasures are given to God's children! May we come to be known for the joy that floods our being. O Lord, may our worship break loose all bonds and may the joy of the Lord fill the earth!

"But let the righteous be glad; let them rejoice before God, yea, let them exceedingly rejoice."

Psalm 68:3

For you shall go out with joy, and be led forth with peace; the mountains and the hills shall break forth before you into singing, and all the trees of the field shall clap their hands."

Isaiah 55:12

Hallelujah!

Chapter 6

THE GOD WE WORSHIP

"Know that the Lord, He is God; it is He who has made us, and not we ourselves; we are His people, and the sheep of His pasture." Psalm 100:3

We need now to consider the nature and attributes of God. Our worship is influenced tremendously by the mental conception we have of Him. Words cannot fully describe the extent of just who God is. We frequently run out of adjectives to use when praising Him. Our language seems too limited to express the magnitude of God. Endless volumes could be written on the subject of the nature of God and, even then, much would be left unsaid. Our goal is to know God more fully and to reflect this increasing revelation in worship. God graciously reveals more and more of Himself as we walk with Him, study Scripture, and commit our lives to His worship.

Earlier I mentioned the word "truth" in regard to worship. Scripture points out that God seeks people who will worship Him in spirit and in truth. (John 4:23-24) Understanding just who God is, therefore, becomes essential. So much misunderstanding and confusion prevails that it is no wonder that worship is often "distant" and "clouded." As Jesus said to the Samaritan woman, "Ye worship ye know not what." (John 4:22) I am afraid that He could make that statement to many churches today! Is the God we worship shrouded in secular or political terms? Is He distant and unreachable? Is He accessible only through some "sacred religious trappings?"

Recently, I was involved in a worship workshop, and we were using music designed to bring children into an experience of meaningful worship. We had broken into small groups and my group was creatively designing hand motions to symbolize key words in a particular song. Things went smoothly until we reached the phrase, "God sends down His rain." There was considerable confusion and disagreement in regard to symbolizing the word, "God." We finally agreed on a symbol, but many of us were not completely comfortable with it. Lofty theological circles are currently grappling with the question of defining "Who is God?" Frankly, I shudder at some of the conclusions that are being reached. (I hope they remember to tell God just whom they have decided Him to be!)

I have spoken with many people who have childhood

memories of entering a cold, dark cathedral type building to "worship." The stark architectural setting, combined with a worship experience lacking joy, warmth, or even a sharing type of love left an indelible impression of a god who is cold, austere, and harsh. God, seen through those eyes, is very unapproachable. Do we view God as a harsh taskmaster who remains distant and who might "strike us down" if we dare venture too close? Many people do view God in those terms. Their "fear of the Lord" is an unhealthy one. Down deep they do not want to draw close to God, they are afraid. This cold view of God is not supported by Scripture and must grieve Him terribly. God wants us to be His people, even His children!

". . . I will put my laws into their mind, and write them in their hearts; and I will be to them a God, and they shall be to Me a people.

And they shall not teach every man his neighbor, and every man his brother, saying, Know the Lord; for all shall know Me, from the least to the greatest." Hebrews 8:10-11

God is no respector of persons. From the least to the greatest His will is that we know Him. He is approachable. He says, "Come unto Me." We, therefore now have "boldness to enter into the holiest by the blood of Jesus." (Hebrews 10:19) God, in Jesus, has made full provision for our reconciliation to Him. Yes, we can enter!

Some people are limited in their understanding of God's mercy, love, compassion, and even His gentleness because their natural father was or is harsh, unloving, or even cruel. Some, also tend to have difficulty relating to the sovereignty of God and the absoluteness and righteousness of His judgments because they view Him through the actions of a father who sets no standards and whose interpretation of "love" denies discipline. What grief and tragedy can result from that kind of situation! God, however, is sovereign and He can and desires to reach out to us, irregardless of our background. The key lies with us. Will we let Him?

> *"Behold, I stand at the door, and knock; if any man hear my voice, and open the door, I will come in to him, and will sup with him, and he with Me."*   *Revelation 3:20*

There is another error in our perception of God which prevails today. This one goes to the other extreme. It brings God down to our level. The "secular religious mentality" dwells here. This is the attempt to define God in terms of our own mental perception. God, then, becomes trapped by our "educated enlightenment" and theological prisons. How often I have heard people and clergy say in lofty terms, "God is like this," or "God is like that," as though Darwin and Freud invented Him and the modern scientific mind needs to put acceptable clothing on Him. The arrogance of the modern mind seems to know no limits.

I once heard a minister state to his congregation that there was no accurate image of God to be found (including the Bible) and therefore they needed to listen to his preaching to enlighten their understanding. (Talk about blind arrogance!) An associate of mine heard that a pastor recommended that his congregation go to a particular modern art gallery to see God. He felt that somehow God could be found in some of the paintings. Is it any wonder that worship is so powerless and confused in so many places?

Many sincere Bible believing Christians also err in trivializing God. Frequently, this stems from an "arrival" theology which somehow gives the impression that at some point we "have it all." (Instant sanctification for the rest of our lives.) Christ has done it all, but we have a daily walk with Him. In the words of Paul, "work out you own salvation with fear and trembling." (Philippians 2:12) We easily slip into a complacent attitude towards God and He becomes our "good ole buddy up in the sky!" This "friend up there" exists then to nod appreciatively on all our pursuits (whether or not they have any direct relation to God or His will) and to shower us with endless blessings if we follow certain prescribed formulas or even Scriptural "encantations." This obviously is a distorted view of God.

Actually, I do sincerely believe that God's provision for His people is abundance. That abundance, however, is related to obedience to His will and concerns sufficiency to meet our needs and those of others. It cannot be applied through legalistic or materialistic eyes. Also, as mentioned earlier, we should never take God's holiness and our need for a continual cleansing in Christ's blood lightly. We must walk in daily obedience.

Recently, I was on a weekend campout with my 7 year old son. At night the group we were with showed some films. One was a cartoon of "The Emperor's New Clothes." Do you remember that story? How much like that many of us are with our mental perceptions of God. There we stand before God, totally naked, yet beaming with pride over our "gorgeous garments." In addition, those who see the nakedness dare not say anything for fear that they will be seen as "stupid" or "uneducated." In the movie an innocent little boy finally started laughing at the emperor's lack of clothing. Then, everyone acknolwedged what they really had seen all along. Perhaps we need more "honest little children" who state sincerely what they actually see.

What then is our God like? In the words of a popular gospel chorus, "How great is our God!" In the words of David:

> "Thine, O Lord, is the greatness, and the power, and the glory, and the victory, and the majesty; for all that is in heaven and the earth is Thine. Thine is the kingdom, O Lord, and Thou art exalted as head above all.
>
> Both riches and honor come of Thee, and Thou reignest over all; and in Thine hand is power and might; and in Thine hand it is to make great, and to give strength to all."
>
> 1 Chronicles 29:11-12

Isn't that fantastic. What more can anyone say to that?! Our response:

> "Now therefore, our God, we thank Thee, and praise Thy glorious name."
>
> 1 Chronicles 29:13

SOVEREIGN RULER OVER ALL THE EARTH

The Lord is the King. He is the Sovereign Ruler over all the earth.

"For the kingdom is the Lord's; and He is the governor among the nations."

Psalm 22:28

"The Lord is King forever and ever..."

Psalm 10:16

"The earth is the Lord's, and the fullness thereof, the world, and they who dwell therein.
For He has founded it upon the seas, and established it upon the floods."

Psalm 24:1-2

"And He shall reign forever and ever."

Revelation 11:15

Let us affirm in our worship that the Lord reigns! He is in control. The kingdom is His and it is an everlasting kingdom. Praise God!

STRENGTH AND MAJESTY

Our God is a God of strength. His power is endless. He is God Almighty. He gives strength to His people. Consider the following Scriptures.

"The Lord reigneth; He is clothed with majesty. The Lord is clothed with strength, wherewith He hath girded Himself."

Psalm 93:1

"Sing unto God, ye kingdoms of the earth; oh, sing praises unto the Lord,

To Him who rides upon the heavens of heavens, which were of old; lo, He does send out His voice, and that a mighty voice.

Ascribe ye strength unto God; His excellency is over Israel, and His strength is in the clouds.

O God, Thou art awe-inspiring out of Thy holy places; the God of Israel is He who gives strength and power unto His people. Blessed be God."

Psalm 68:32-35

"Honor and majesty are before Him; strength and beauty are in His sanctuary."

Psalm 96:6

Indeed, the place of worship is a place of beauty and a place of strength! Does that inspire you to fall down before God and worship? It does me!

"Bless the Lord, O my soul. O Lord my God, Thou art very great; Thou art clothed with honor and majesty,"
Psalm 104:1

Jesus, "Who, being the brightness of His glory, and the express image of His person, and upholding all things by the word of His power, when He had by Himself purged our sins, sat down on the right hand of the *Majesty* on high." (Hebrews 1:3) And Peter said, "We were eyewitnesses of His (Christ's) majesty." (2 Peter 1:16)

Our God is ruler over all the earth. He is clothed in strength and majesty! Let us bow down before Him. Let us wonder in joy, awe, and thanksgiving at such a God, so great and powerful and yet One who loves us so very much!

"All nations whom Thou hast made shall come and worship before Thee, O Lord, and shall glorify Thy name.
For Thou art great, and doest wondrous things; Thou art God alone."
Psalm 86:9-10

CREATOR

When we worship God, we acknowledge that He is the Creator of the universe. He has made us and we are His.

"In the beginning God created the heaven and the earth."
Genesis 1:1

Do you realize that the above Scripture is the very first verse in the Bible? I can think of no aspect of God's nature more despised and rejected by modern man than that of Creator. How we have bowed down to the idol of Darwinism! "God the Creator? Don't be absurd!" scoffs the secular man. I assure you of this fact: Until you acknowledge God as Creator, you will most likely have a very limited knowledge (and experience) of His power! When the scoffers and cynics stand before God, I believe they too will bow before Him in the fullness of His being. A worshipper in Spirit and truth affirms God as Creator!

> "By the word of the Lord were the heavens made, and all the host of them by the breath of His mouth.
>
> He gathereth the waters of the sea together as an heap; He layeth up the depth in storehouses.
>
> Let all the earth fear the Lord; let all the inhabitants of the world stand in awe of Him.
>
> For He spoke and it was done; He commanded, and it stood fast."
>
> Psalm 33:6-9

By grasping the revelation of God as Creator, we begin to sense the infinite splendor of His power. He creates, He controls, He reigns! He has created us and (this is essential to grasp) He knows us to the very fibre of our being. We cannot escape God. (Psalm 139 and Hebrews 4:13) What comfort it is to go before God, our Maker, who knows and understands the joys, dreams, and burdens of our hearts even before we speak them.

"Before I formed thee in the womb, I knew thee; . . ."
Jeremiah 1:5

As Peter said, "Lord, Thou knowest all things." (John 21:17) Since He is our creator and since He knows us intimately, He is the true source for inspiration and creativity.

"For Thou wilt light my lamp; the Lord, my God, will lighten my darkness."
Psalm 18:28

"The Lord is my light and my salvation; . . ."
Psalm 27:1

"For in Him we live, and move, and have our being; . . ."
Acts 17:28

It is no wonder that contemporary art forms wander aimlessly in search of truth. They reflect a sense of despair, fragmentation, and futile searching. Only when we know the source of truth, the God of Creation, do we have a valid reference point to enrich understanding and to lend beauty and meaning to creativity. For too long art forms have attempted to glorify themselves or the mind and abilities of their human creator. This has even affected art and music used in the church. God knows the intent of our hearts. Do we dare offer Him works of the flesh? Do we dare flaunt our intellects, talents, abilities, and gifts (even those God-given) before Him as though He should be impressed and honored? May we kneel humbly before our Maker in all that we do!

HOLY

Twice before in this book we have discussed the word "holy" in relation to worship. The emphasis here is on affirming the fact that God is Holy.

"Who is like unto Thee, O Lord, among the gods? Who is like Thee, glorious in holiness, fearful in praises, doing wonders?"

Exodus 15:11

This aspect of God's nature is so utterly important. Worship must affirm God's holiness. We live in an unholy age. Man attempts to place himself, not God, in the center of the universe. Religious minds offer God worship that is pleasing to the mind, but not necessarily pleasing to God. In addition, so often we enter into worship with a spirit of apathy. Worship becomes plastic and routine. Do we dare continue to offer Him such a blemished lamb? Let us reflect on the account of the transfiguration.

"And after six days Jesus took Peter, James, and John, His brother, and brought them up into an high mountain privately,

And was transfigured before them; and His face did shine like the sun, and His raiment was

94

as white as the light.

And, behold, there appeared unto them Moses and Elijah talking with Him.

Then answered Peter, and said unto Jesus, Lord, it is good for us to be here; if Thou wilt, let us make here three booths; one for Thee, and one for Moses, and one for Elijah.

While he yet spoke, behold, a bright cloud overshadowed them; and, behold, a voice out of the cloud, which said, This is My beloved Son, in whom I am well pleased; hear ye Him.

And when the disciples heard it, they fell on their face, and were very much afraid.

And Jesus came and touched them, and said, Arise, and be not afraid."   Matthew 17:1-7

It is awesome and frightening to see God face to face. And yet, Jesus reached down, touched them, and said, "Be not afraid." So it is with us. A gentle, beauteous voice beckons us to "come near." As we enter, we experience a blessed quietness, a flowing peace. It is something wonderfully pure and clean, and yet there is a sense of wholeness, fulfillment, belonging, destiny. "Lord, let us make booths," we plead. But the Lord says, "Refresh your souls in My still waters, walk in My green pastures, but then go in My love. Share My truth. Freely give My compassion." We are changed. Our lives can never quite be the same. We go in obedience. But, we cherish the golden bond that exists when we come together with others who also have known the summit and others who, with sincere and hungry hearts, yearn to go there with us.

"The Lord is in His holy temple; let all the earth keep silence before Him."

Habakkuk 2:20

GOD IS MERCIFUL

"Oh, give thanks unto the Lord, for He is good; because His mercy endureth forever."

Psalm 118:1

Mercy is that quality of forgoing retribution even when punishment is due. Once again, we are confronted with the staggering reality of a God, all knowing, all powerful, Who alone is just and holy, and yet Who reaches out to us with love and forgiveness. God is merciful! This is something to which we can hold on. How often we find ourselves in dark and ominous situations of our own making. In times such as these our only hope is God. We know He is faithful and can be trusted. (Psalm 36:5) We find ourselves cast upon His grace and our faith rests in the fact that He is merciful. Praise God for that!

"But I am like a green olive tree in the house of God; I trust in the mercy of God forever and ever."

Psalm 52:8

God's mercy is affirmed throughout Scripture. Consider the following verses.

"But Thou art a God ready to pardon, gracious and merciful, slow to anger, and of great kindness, . . ."   *Nehemiah 9:17*

". . . for I am merciful, saith the Lord, and I will not keep anger forever."   *Jeremiah 3:12*

"But God, who is rich in mercy, for His great love with which He loved us,"
Ephesians 2:4

And finally, as said by Mary,

"For He that is mighty hath done to me great things; and holy is His name.
And His mercy is on them that fear Him from generation to generation."   *Luke 1:49-50*

Let us glorify God because He is merciful to us. Let us pray that His mercy flows through us and out in compassionate love to others. (Luke 6:36) As we are called to be God's people, let us not only bear testimony in our lives to His holiness, but let us shed His mercy abroad throughout the earth! Our acts of mercy performed in love and obedience to the Lord bring honor and glory to Him. This is yet another vital form of worship! Malcolm Muggeridge in his book,

"Something Beautiful For God,"[1] tells of Mother Theresa's mission of mercy and compassion to the hopeless and dying in Calcutta. There, God's peace and love is given sacrificially to the "unlovely" people who have starved, been homeless, and known nothing but severe deprivation. It is especially poignant to read of the compassion and care given to those dying.

I recall one incident in the book which remained with me. A large room was filmed where the terminally ill were placed. This room was very dark and it was feared that the film would not turn out. However, when the film was developed, a heavenly radiance appeared illuminating the room. The expert cameraman in charge had absolutely no natural explanation for the source of this light! May the light of Christ shine in and through us! Let us be merciful. Let us worship the God of mercy.

"I will sing of the mercies of the Lord forever; with my mouth will I make known Thy faithfulness to all generations."

Psalm 89:1

"GOD IS LOVE" (1 John 4:8)

The word "love" is so overused and misused today that it has lost much of its strength and power. The world views love in terms of emotional feeling, sexual attractiveness and gratification, and general fondness for or appreciation of

[1]Malcom Muggeridge, *Something Beautiful For God* (New York, Image Books, 1977)

something. Just as society has tended to define God in its own terms and thereby attempted to "trivialize" Him, so with love. Oh, how we overuse that word. Try standing for God's truth in society or even in church circles and listen to the cries of the people to be "loving." What are they saying? Is it loving to deny God? Is it being loving to suppress His truth? Is it being loving to diminish the light He has given? Absolutely not! We need to be very careful in our use and interpretation of that word.

Love is based on truth, it requires understanding, and it demands obedience and sacrifice. Love does not come cheaply. It bears a definite cost. Love is a decision. That may sound strange but it is true. You see, love bears great responsibility. Our society says, "Enjoy love! Give free reign to your appetites and emotions and don't be 'hung up' by antiquated feelings of guilt or responsibility. After all, we have been 'liberated' from the cumbersome restrictions of religion." How incredible is the tragedy, despair, and depravity this trail leaves. The fruits of society's "pop" definition of love are perverse licentiousness and fearful fragmentation. Love, then, is based on a decision to know the truth, to be obedient to the truth, and to stand firm to those commitments even at personal cost and sacrifice.

Love thus becomes "heroic." This is a word quite out of vogue today. To sacrifice oneself for a higher cause, for truth, is viewed with great cynicism. God's love for us is costly, sacrificial, and heroic. In fact, those words somehow fall short of the magnitude of it. Several examples from literature stand out in my mind.

Who can forget the sad figure, named Sydney Carton, in Dicken's "Tale of Two Cities." His life was one of futility, absense of real meaning, and aimlessness. My heart still stirs as I recollect his walk to the guillotine in place of Charles Darnay, a good and righteous man. In death, Sydney Carton found meaning. He, in his decision to lay down his life for another, experienced something higher.

I also recall a troubled, tragic figure from "Les Miserables" named Jean Valjean. Escaped from prison, from an unduly harsh sentence, he wandered to the home of a godly man, Bishop Bienvenu. The Bishop received him with compassion and kindness. How did Jean Valjean respond? Years of imprisonment had taken their toll. He left in the night and stole the Bishop's six silver plates. The authorities caught him and when they brought him before Monsignor Bienvenu, the Bishop said that he gave the plates to Valjean and he then added six precious candlesticks to the plates. Jean Valjean was filled with wonder and confusion. Why? He thought. The Bishop said to him, "Jean Valjean, my brother, you belong no longer to evil, but to good. It is your soul that I am buying for you. I withdraw it from dark thoughts and from the spirit of perdition, and I give it to God."

Jesus said, "He that loseth his life for my sake shall find it." (Matthew 10:39) "Except a grain of wheat fall into the ground and die, it abideth alone; but if it die, it bringeth forth much fruit." (John 12:24) "Greater love hath no man than this, that a man lay down his life for his friends." (John 15:13)

This is the love that the world hungers for. This is God's love. This is the love that is offered to us in Jesus, who died for us! (John 3:16) This is the love, made real in sacrificial action, that brings fulfillment, freedom, and gives real life to others. You see, we may choose to live life to the fullest, as God teaches us, or we may choose to clutch on to ourselves, our ambitions, our desire for self-fulfillment, and our craving for pleasure and gratification. God's love is costly, but it is true. It brings liberty. Today, we break off and terminate relationships rather than suffer a personal cost. God's love may send us through the fire, but He will be there with us. As we emerge, there will not even be "the smell of smoke upon us." (Daniel 3)

A worshipper affirms God's love. A worshipper is a doer of the word. Let me share a parable with you.

Once there were two young men, "Zealous" and "Also Ran." Zealous symbolized accomplishment and achievement. His life bore testimony to hard work, accomplishment, and success. He set his goals, worked diligently, and achieved the desired results. People looked up to Zealous. Also Ran, however, was a different story. He never could quite make it in life. He was not very attractive. He was only average in mental and physical abilities. He could never quite figure things out and put it all together. He knew failure much better than success. In fact, he had failed so often that he had just about quit trying.

The time was approaching for the big marathon race. Zealous had looked forward to this race for years. He had trained conscientiously and had earnestly coveted the particular trophy which would be awarded to the winner. Also Ran was not really sure how he became entered in this race. He really had no hope of winning. He knew that it would most likely bring yet another defeat to him. Nevertheless, he seemed to sense a quiet voice saying, "Try one more time." He did not understand it but he found himself signing up.

The day of the race finally arrived. Spectators lined up along the course to witness the action. Most, however, gathered at the finish line. A sense of excitement and anticipation filled the air. The gun sounded and the race was on! The runners raced up and down hill after hill, around corners, and down long streets. As the race progressed, many runners fell back or dropped out.

Strangely, rounding the last turn and going into the final mile, only two runners could be seen. They were Zealous and Also Ran. Zealous was doing fine. He was about 20 yards in front and felt very strong. He could sense that familiar smell of victory. After all, he had worked for it, he deserved it, and now it would be his! Also Ran had given absolutely everything he had. He did not know why but this race seemed especially important. It was his final try. Now, however, he was exhausted and he glanced with anguished fatigue at the hill leading up to the finish line.

The crowd was beginning to cheer. Zealous, feeling very confident, looked back over his shoulder quickly to see just how large his lead was. As he glanced back, something very strange happened. He felt something deep down in his heart. An incredible thought seemed to fill his mind and body. He resisted it and wrestled mentally for what seemed like a long time. Suddenly, to the wonder of the crowd, his pace slackened. Also Ran gradually caught up with him and gave him a confused look. Zealous then turned to Also Ran and said with a peace and assurance of voice, "Go ahead! Press on. Take the trophy. It is yours." Also Ran surged ahead like a man with new life and he crossed the finish line. Zealous finished right behind him and felt a new strength. His entire body seemed flooded with a strange, wonderful warmth. Truly, "many are called, but few chosen." (Matthew 20:16)

God is Love. May we shout it from the housetops. May we declare it boldly in our lives. May we worship Him for it.

"But He knows the way that I take; when He has tested me, I shall come forth as gold."

Job 23:10(NIV)

GLORY AND SPLENDOR

"For Thine is the kingdom, and the power, and the glory forever." — *Matthew 6:13*

Oh, how I love this subject! God is glorious, reigning in splendor. The word "glory" is used so often in Scripture in reference to God that one could fill a book just listing those references! Let's look at a few.

"Lift up your heads, O ye gates; and be ye lifted up, ye everlasting doors; and the King of glory shall come in.

Who is this King of glory? The Lord strong and mighty, the Lord mighty in battle.

Lift up your heads, O ye gates; even lift them up, ye everlasting doors; and the King of glory shall come in.

Who is this King of glory: The Lord of hosts, He is the King of glory."

Psalm 24:7-10

When Jesus was born, an angel of the Lord appeared to shepherds watching their flocks "and the glory of the Lord

103

shone round about them." (Luke 2:9)

> "And suddenly there was with the angel a multitude of the heavenly host, praising God, and saying,
>
> Glory to God in the highest, and on earth peace, good will toward men."
>
> Luke 2:13-14

While on earth Jesus reflected His Father's glory.

> "And the Word was made flesh, and dwelt among us (and we beheld His glory, the glory as of the only begotten of the Father,) full of grace and truth."
>
> John 1:14

It was prophesied that in the Messiah, "the glory of the Lord shall be revealed." (Isaiah 40:5) Jesus was described as being "the brightness of the Father's glory." (Hebrews 1:3) Jesus' life reflected God's glory and He sought to glorify His Father in the ministry given to Him. (John 17:1,4) Now, Jesus is "at the right hand of glory." (Acts 7:55) And, "He will come again in glory." (Luke 21:27)

Picture with me the risen, glorified Christ as He appeared to John on the isle of Patmos.

> "And I turned to see the voice that spoke with me. And being turned, I saw seven golden lampstands,

And in the midst of the seven lampstands one like the Son of Man, clothed with a garment down to the foot, and girded about the breasts with a golden girdle.

His head and His hair were white like wool, as white as snow; and His eyes were like a flame of fire;

And His feet like fine bronze, as if they burned in a furnace; and His voice like the sound of many waters.

And He had in His right hand seven stars; and out of His mouth went a sharp two-edged sword; and His countenance was as the sun shines in its strength.

And when I saw Him, I fell at His feet as dead. And He laid His right hand upon me, saying unto me, Fear not; I am the first and the last;

I am He that liveth, and was dead; and, behold, I am alive for evermore, Amen."

Revelation 1:12-18

That is quite a different picture than the one of the gentle shepherd pictured in Sunday school books! Notice also the similarities between John's response and in Jesus' words to him and the account of the transfiguration previously cited. Let us also reflect on the glory of God and the worship pictured in the culmination of history.

"And every creature that is in heaven, and on the earth, and under the earth, and such as are in the sea, and all that are in them, heard I saying, Blessing, and honor, and glory, and power be unto Him that sitteth upon the throne, and unto the Lamb forever and ever. Revelation 5:13-14

"And the temple was filled with smoke from the glory of God, and from His power;" Revelation 15:8

Dear Christian, that is worship! And in the heavenly city:

"And the city has no need of the sun, neither of the moon, to shine in it, for the glory of God did light it, and the Lamb is the lamp of it." Revelation 22:23

The glory of the Lord is a wondrous thing to ponder, . . . to behold, . . . to share. Do our lives reflect His glory? Does our worship bear witness to His glory and power? Are we really only giving "lip service" to the glory of God? God wants us to know and behold His glory. (2 Cor.4:6) He wants His glory to shine in and through us. (2 Cor. 3:18) Isn't that absolutely fantastic! Therefore, with infinite joy, let us give glory to God! Let us cry out in worship of Him! He is glorious!

". . . and in His temple everything cries out, "Glory!" (author's paraphrase)   Psalm 29:9

And may everything in our earthly temples also say, "Glory!"

Chapter 7

AN HONEST LOOK AT OUR WORSHIP

"Examine me, O Lord, and prove me; test my heart and my mind."   *Psalm 26:2*

"And unto the church write: I know thy works . . ."   *Revelation 2*

It is very difficult to assess our private and corporate worship honestly. We often have quite a few "sacred cows."

In addition, we run into so many people who seem to specialize in "fault finding" that we are leery of being accused of possessing a critical spirit. It serves no purpose to find error merely to delight in being critical. The fact is, however, that God wants worship in spirit and truth. Whether we like it or not, He will judge all of our works, even those performed unto Him. (Genesis 4) His interest is in sincerity and purity of heart, not our precious "religious trappings", sensitivities, or pride. As if this were not sufficient reason to examine our worship closely, consider this: God's will is for us to partake of His full portion, Why settle for less? To do so is like refusing to be seated at the most bountiful feast imaginable because we are unsure of our invitation or too proud to pull out our chair and sit down! (Actually, some may go so far as to sit down at the table and then still refuse to partake because they just cannot bring themselves to believe that the incredible spread of food is really offered to them.) Let us, therefore, with the clear vision of pressing on into the fullness of God's presence and will, sincerely assess the worship we offer to God and share with each other.

PRESENTS THE TRUE PICTURE OF GOD

First, let us reflect on the nature and attributes of God as previously discussed. Does our worship truly glorify God? Or does it, instead, glorify the leaders or celebrants? Are we putting on a big "program" or "show" for our own pleasure? Let me interject a brief comment. Worship does not need to have a "cast of thousands" (or an accompaniment tape with a cast of thousands) to be glorious. Big does not necessarily mean better. God is looking at the hearts of the worshippers, not the grandeur of the production. Are the powerful words of scripture recited, heard, and sung coming from the heart or are we blandly mouthing phrases? I know that may sound harsh to some of you. I can only say, however, that I recently attended a worship service where some of the most poignant scriptures relating to the greatness of God were recited. The words were hopelessly lost in the magnitude of the "worship production," and they seemed to race across everyone's ears and pass on by. Once again, let us humbly examine our priorities and what is actually being accomplished. Let us not treat worship lightly. Let us never lose sight of God in the flurry of putting on some grand performance.

Does our worship present a true and balanced picture of God? This is an essential initial guidepost. Does it affirm and reflect His utter holiness and His infinite love, mercy, and compassion? Does it also affirm and reflect His righteousness and judgments? His grace?

BASED ON PROPER RELATIONSHIPS

Is our worship based on proper relationships? Jesus said, "I am the way, the truth, and the life; no man comes unto the Father, but by Me." (John 14:6) Does our worship begin with the affirmation of this crucial fact? We may be flooded with gorgeous music, spell-bound by magnificent architecture, and held in breath-taking awe by eloquent preaching; but, if we are "soft pedaling" or ignoring the need for redemption and reconciliation through Jesus, His life-death-and resurrection, we are offering God worship that is unacceptable. All of us make mistakes and occasionally act out of ignorance. But, there is no excuse for members of the Church of Jesus Christ coming to God in worship without passing through "the Door of the sheep!" (John 10:7-9)

In addition to our relationship with Jesus, are we obediently fulfilling God's will in other relationships? Do we approach our brothers and sisters in Christ in a spirit of brokenness and humility or do we operate with indifference, arrogance, or self-interest? Earlier I mentioned the need for lasting bonds between Christians. Again we ask, "How deep are our wells?" (or, "How shallow are our cisterns?") Are we really going before God in worship with bitterness or unforgiveness in our hearts? (We may have every reason to be angry and unforgiving but, we dare not try to worship God in that spirit! Mark 11:25-26)

COMPASSION TO OTHERS

Do we come before God as servants willing to be obedient to His word? Are our hearts filled with compassion? Do we reach out to others with His saving truth and caring love? This is all part of balance in our Christian journey. Worship can be quite edifying but it is out of balance if we have no concern (shown in action) for the hungry, poor, and needy. We need to make certain that our hearts have not become hardened and complacent to the voices crying out for help, for hope, for life. Do we care in tangible ways for the hungry, the poor, the elderly, the infirm, the unwanted, the disabled, the unborn? We cannot do everything, but we need to, out of our love for Jesus and in obedience to God's word, try to do something. God's word speaks directly to this.

"I hate, I despise your feast days, and I will not take delight in your solemn assemblies.
Though you offer me burnt offerings and your meal

111

offerings, I will not accept them; neither will I regard the peace offerings of your fat beasts.

Take away from me the noise of thy songs; for I will not hear the melody of thine harps.

But let justice run down like waters, and righteousness like a mighty stream."

Amos 5:21-24

It is a privilege to share Christ with others and to reach out in love to those in need. It is futility to do this apart from Christ. It is insincere to worship God without a compassionate, caring heart. We have the gospel of the Kingdom to proclaim in word and deed. Our worship should reflect our obedience to our heavenly calling.

PARTICIPATION

Another important factor to consider in assessing our worship is the area of participation. Does our corporate worship involve and encourage participation? Do the people really participate? Are the hymns sung with power and conviction or are they feeble and weak in sound?

Many people feel that the mere act of attending a worship service suffices. Their presence equals participation. Is that true? Does sitting in the stadium mean that you are participating in the game? Nowadays, it is quite possible to sit in a padded pew and observe a worship performance by capable professionals and trained leaders. We listen to fine musical soloists. We hear the choir perform. We listen to a well written sermon delivered artistically. We sit, we listen, we watch. We have entered into a performer/audience relationship. Is this worship? I believe it to be a throwback to the Middle Ages where certain priests "celebrated" worship while the public quietly sat and observed. Worship was considered to be so "holy" that the "laity" (try to find that word in scripture!) were not allowed to participate. They sat passively and viewed the proceedings.

Today, we have placed such emphasis on "professionalism" in regard to performance that training and expertise are sought and valued highly. This is often carried to the extreme position of relegating the "laity" to the familiar role of "observer." They are there to appreciate, not necessarily to participate. Naturally, gifts and abilities will stand out. However, we need to channel those gifts and abilities into encouraging and helping others to freely participate in the worship experience. Worship must be viewed as a shared act of devotion by the entire Christian family. I recently viewed a video tape of a noted Christian recording artist performing in a church. He was supposed to be leading them in worship. What I saw, however, was him playing his music to an elaborate pre-recorded background. The entire performance was broadcast through an extensive sound system. The people, though, were standing in a confused manner wondering what they were supposed to do. Were they to hum along? Were they to clap? Were they to stand and look? The music was well done, but it was not corporate worship. Worship involves participation, meaningful participation, by all. Does our worship allow and promote that?

BALANCE IN THE ELEMENTS

We need to make sure that our worship makes a balanced

use of all of the elements (prayer, praise, music, confession, preaching, affirmation of faith, etc.) Preaching the word, for example, is an essential part of practically all worship services. Some suggest, however, that we have gone too far in this direction. Indeed, listening to a gifted speaker proclaiming the word is something needed and quite exciting. But, worship is more than just sitting and listening to a sermon, no matter how eloquent the speaker may be.

Some time ago I attended worship at a church that followed this general form: Opening hymn, several printed prayers recited by the congregation, sermon, offering and anthem, closing prayer read by clergy, and closing hymn. That really sounds very normal and typical, doesn't it. The main problem (and there were others) was that the sermon took 40 minutes of the 1 hour service. In addition, the congregational participation was tightly controlled and a general feeling of "lifelessness" was present. I distinctly recall feeling a little like a "caged bird." I wanted to praise God and pray; to sing and share with others; to hear their joys and concerns expressed before God; and to prayerfully intercede with them and together offer thanksgiving to God. In short, I wanted to enter into worship with them. Regretfully, there seemed to be no opportunity. The service was on time and tightly planned. Unfortunately, there just did not seem to be enthusiasm or life.

We place a high emphasis on organizational skills. Because of this there is a tendency to think that a rigidly controlled, "polished" worship service is a good one. Personally, I would gladly sacrifice the "polish" for life and vitality. Of course, we are partly spoiled by the broadcast media. All we have to do is flick on the switch and we can hear outstanding speakers, professional choirs (with plenty of rehearsal), and the best in religious music (complete with overdubbing, splicing, and hours at the "mixing" booth.) The closer we get to this "professional" sound, the more spiritual we think it is. As one who performed music professionally for years, let me assure you that even though we strive for quality in worship, professionalism can be terribly dead! Polish does not mean life.

PRAYER, CONFESSION, CREEDS

We need to seriously reflect on the entire spectrum of worship. This should include a sensitive evaluation of the various types of prayers, confessions, and creeds used. Are they meaningful? Do the people actually participate wholly in them or do they merely mouth words? Is there flexibility and diversity in implementation? Are we locked into only one particular form?

There are many ways prayer could be shared in worship. We could have a participant read a prayer. We could all share in responsive prayers, or, we may join in silent or spontaneous prayers. I find it extremely beneficial to use a variety of types of prayers. A worship leader, for example, might read prayers from past generations and end with a new or original prayer. Also, he might read a prayer and allow time for the congregation to voice spontaneous prayers on the same theme. The possibilities are many and varied. The questions remain. "Does your worship promote, allow, and encourage meaningful prayer? Do all have a chance to share?"

Confession, as with prayer, offers many possibilities. As worshippers, we need an opportunity to go before God and be cleansed. This should not be taken lightly. We can use written confessions, silent ones, or in some cases, spontaneous ones. Being cleansed of sin is a joyful experience. Do we take it too lightly? Is it part of a dull routine? Do we realize the content of what is transpiring?

Finally, we come to creeds. There are many and they all attempt to define our faith. This question must be asked. "Do the worshippers really understand and affirm in their hearts the truths being spoken?" This is essential.

It may sound strange, but I have shared in worship where people recited statements in creeds that they really did not believe in. A creed is a vital testimony of what we believe. It is not a meaningless religious ritual. Does the creed have relevance and truth to your family of worshippers?

SACRAMENTS

While some sacraments are affirmed and celebrated more than others, all churches celebrate Baptism and the Lord's Supper.

Essentially, a Sacrament presents a truth so important and relevant to our faith that we affirm it physically in genuine participation. In our worship, do we feel and realize the solemnity and importance of this sacred act? (This does not rule out joyful celebration!) Has it become routine and casual? A Sacrament is a holy act performed in the presence of a holy God and has lasting significance. Sadly, Christians often treat them with attitudes that border on apathy and disrespect. Is this true in your worship?

Sacraments, in addition to affirming lasting truth and covenants, bring the body together in realization of common commitment and purpose. They reveal and foster a sense of being called into a "holy body". Is this realization acknowledged in our worship?

Communion is one Sacrament that needs to be specifically discussed. Jesus, Himself, instituted it (Matthew 26:26-29) and it has profound meaning. It is an act of remembrance (1 Corinthians 11:25) and also celebration. Jesus indicated a glorious feast in His Father's Kingdom (Matthew 26:29) and we shall partake with Him! We remember and celebrate Christ's death and resurrection and we look to His coming again in glory! (1 Corinthians 11:25-26)

In the Sacrament of the Lord's Supper, we also recognize and affirm our place and participation in Christ's Body, the church. (1 Corinthians 10:16-17) Does our celebration of this Sacrament affirm these things? Do we partake of the Table of the Lord too seldom? Has it become routine? Do we share it in an unworthy manner? Are our hearts right with God and with each other? Do we sense the infinite holiness and grace of God as we partake?

The outward form of celebration is not the most essential feature. The heart is! I have shared in Eucharistic services in homes where the cup and bread were passed from Christian to Christian, in churches where the Sacrament was received seated in pews, and in cathedrals where one stood or knelt in the front of the sanctuary. Is there flexibility and meaning in the way we participate? As we celebrate this Divine feast, do we draw close to God and to each other? Has even this holy Sacrament become in our particular practice a religious museum piece? (God forbid!)

Finally, I must state that Holy Communion is an extremely meaningful area for creativity in music. Does the music presented both affirm God's grace and inspire us? Does it speak gently to us of love, brokenness, and consecration? Does it reach us? Does it add to the holiness of this sacred event?

117

SPONTANEITY

Spontaneity is closely related to participation. The word "spontaneity" frightens many people. It is sometimes felt that something unexpected and perhaps shocking will happen. This is not what is really meant by spontaneity in worship.

In the first place, worship that is inspired and led by the Holy Spirit rarely is "shocking." Furthermore, there is a flow and a common thread woven in the worship experience. It may, however, be quite spontaneous. There are two definitions of spontaneity in regard to worship.

The first is this: An increased sense of personal participation. In this context spontaneity means that there is an openness in our form of worship or in places in our service where an individual could become involved in a personal way, if he or she so chooses. The question we must ask ourselves then is whether or not our worship allows such personal participation. Perhaps it is a time of sharing. Perhaps it is spontaneous or even silent prayer. Perhaps at an appropriate time someone begins to sing a hymn or chorus and others join in. Maybe someone has a scripture to share that is meaningful and pertinent. It must be pointed out that mere scheduling does not make spontaneity. If the worship is tightly controlled or dominated in spirit by one or more strong, authoritarian type leaders, chances are that there will be only a token sense of personal participation. This will be the case even if the bulletin "commands" participation.

I must share with you my experience in giving worship workshops. At some point the issue of spontaneity is addressed. Frequently, we will have the participants add their own verses to songs. In any event, when the people begin to share in a spontaneous way, a real joy manifests itself and things really start to "take off." As mentioned earlier, I have traditionally been a fairly inhibited type person. Learning to be spontaneous in worship has brought great personal release and freedom. It gives liberty and fosters tremendous creativity in expressing praise to God.

The other definition of spontaneity that I like is "planned creativity." Just by the brief list of things mentioned earlier (prayer, music, etc.) we can begin to see the many possibilities for facilitating spontaneity. We use our planning to creatively set the stage for personal participation and then we let the Holy Spirit lead and inspire! The question remains, "Does our worship allow room for spontaneity?" If the answer is no, we may have closed some very important doors into the exciting and dynamic presence and movement of the Holy Spirit in our worship.

CREATIVE/ECLECTIC

Is our worship creative? Does it reflect the richness and diversity of God the Creator? Does it reflect the richness and diversity of the people with whom we share worship? Does it inspire and motivate individuals to "stretch out" and try new things? Or is it predicatble and routine? I have attended both "structured" and "free" type worship services where a freshness and a high degree of inspiration and creativity were exhibited. Also, I have endured both forms of worship services that did not. In some services the same songs and the same prayers are offered at the same place week after week. Vitality and life quickly fade in this type of setting. On the other hand, we must make sure that our creativity is sensitive to the direction and leading of the Holy Spirit. Creativity done merely for the sake of variety or being different can be quite hollow.

Some years ago I was asked to be involved in an early morning "contemporary" worship service on a weekly basis. I should have been on guard at the use of the word "contemporary." Nevertheless, I said yes, and participated for quite some time. It became increasingly apparent that the purpose of the service was to satisfy those individuals who wanted change for the sake of change. Just about everything was thrown in, (including pop tunes from the top forty and secular readings!) It was not good. I quickly learned that this was not the way to be creative or "relevant." We must never lose the vision of offering a holy sacrifice of worship, pleasing and acceptable to our holy God.

Eclectic is a valuable word. Although I had heard this word used from time to time, I never gave it much thought until one particular incident occurred. My father is known throughout the world for the guitar teaching books and methods he has written and because of this, he is always receiving interesting things in the mail. One day a friend of ours sent us an original copy of a guitar method printed and published in the 1800's. The rather unique title was, "The Eclectic Guitar Method." (Yes, it really said "eclectic," not "electric.") As I leafed carefully through the yellowed pages, I remember commenting, "The music looks interesting, but it surely wouldn't go anywhere with that title!" I then started thinking about the word "eclectic" and realized that I did not know much about its meaning. As I looked it up I discovered that it meant "to draw the best from a variety of sources." In worship, therefore, eclectic can be a very valuable word.

Not only is there richness in worship forms as practiced

by Christians in different denominations, but there is a treasure of resources dating back into church history and emerging at the present time. An eclectic approach to worship will, under the leading of the Holy Spirit, draw from the vast storehouse of music, liturgy, prayer, etc., both old and new, and use what is valid. These items will then be applied with a freshness, vitality, and dedication to quality. The criteria for usage become: "Is it good? Is it true? Is it relevant to what the Lord is saying to us? Can we use it effectively? Will it glorify the Lord and edify the congregation?" We pause and reflect on these questions. "Is our worship creative? Does it reflect God's richness and diversity? Is it both eclectic and meaningful?"

QUALITY

We have briefly touched on this aspect of worship earlier in the book. Quality is essential. We must make every effort to offer to God the very best. How much time do we spend preparing for worship? Is that time quality time? These questions need to be answered by all participants in worship.

What about prayer? How much time is spent in prayer prior to worship? Are we just going through the motions and relying on planning and organizational skills and experience or do we humbly travail before God for His will, guidance, and blessing? Let me state as strongly as I can that anyone involved in planning and leading worship must know God and spend time with Him in prayer! Prayer is vital! Without it we risk going before God in a spirit of presumption. This also applies to individual worship. In fact, it is a required prerequisite!

Most worship committees spend precious few moments in

prayer before "getting on with the business at hand." This is not the way to plan worship. If we spend quality time together seeking and waiting on God, our meetings have direction and they seem to flow with His anointing and blessing. We must take God, worship, and prayer seriously. It is not the amount of time spent, but the quality of time. Our minds and hearts cannot be preoccupied with other matters or cold with boredom and indifference. We cannot expect guidance through prayer if we are not sincerely attempting to be "one in the Spirit." Contentions, anger, bitterness, resentments must be done away with prior to seeking God's blessing and guidance in worship. God demands the best. Is He worthy of any less? Let us get our hearts right with Him.

Once we have spent time on our knees before God, we are then ready to spend the time needed to make other preparations. I used to think that rehearsal was somehow "unspiritual." That is a wrong assumption. Only when we really know our parts do we have the freedom to express ourselves fully through whatever medium with which we are involved (music, readings, prayers, preachings, etc.)

I frequently tell musicians, "Only after you know your instrument thoroughly and have mastered the music to be played are you free and able to express your feelings and personality through this medium." Once again, the heart must be right. I have endured countless rehearsals conducted purely in technical and fleshly terms. During these practice sessions the music is often performed in a cold, detached manner. The result may be correct musically, but is there real love and passion in it? Does it sing out to God?

Give me a choir that spends time (yes, even rehearsal time) in prayer, worshipping God, and I will show you a choir that sings with Godly intensity and sensitivity. That is the choir with which I choose to share worship. The only musical credentials God honors are gifts and abilities wholly sanctified unto Him through deep love of heart.

We need a commitment to quality. How often we give the Lord second best. How frequently we offer Him surface level commitment and "sacrifice" that bears little real cost. How little time we spend in prayer and preparation for worshipping our mighty and holy God. Let us have hearts on fire for God and quality worship. Both go together!

INTER-GENERATIONAL/BUILDING FAMILY

Does our worship allow meaningful participation for all age groups? Does it relate to both young and old? Do we foster the feeling of being together in the family of God? This does not suggest that you must have a children's number, an old hymn or gospel song, etc. each week. We do, however, need to be sensitive to the various ages present in worship. To totally exclude children or the elderly, for example, from meaningful participation and understanding of worship is a tragic mistake. There is no generation gap with God, unless we create one "in His name."

Some of the most poignant memories I have of worship gatherings are those where a genuine participation occurs and real love is shown between people of all ages. It is possible and quite wonderful. What pleasure I feel when one of my boys talks to me about a worship service with joy and enthusiasm. I also recall the warmth we, as parents, feel inside when our children go to bed singing a praise-oriented song heard in worship. I, also, have many fond memories of elderly people, with their eyes sparkling with enthusiasm, telling me how much they appreciated a piece of music shared in worship.

We must never forget that we are a family, God's family. Worship should draw us together, heal wounds, bind hurts, and bring about understanding, forgiveness, reconciliation, and love. No matter how intellectual, eloquent, or gifted he may be, a worship leader must have a pastoral love for the people of God. The world offers isolation and fragmentation while it exalts "the gifted." The church of Jesus Christ must give wholeness and acceptance. His loving light must replace the world's cold, barren darkness.

"Behold, how good and how pleasant it is for brethren to dwell together in unity!

It is like the precious ointment upon the head, that ran down upon the beard, even Aaron's beard; that went down to the skirts of his garments,

Like the dew of Hermon, and like the dew that descended upon the mountains of Zion; for there the Lord commanded the blessing, even life for evermore."   *Psalm 133*

EDIFYING

When we worship, we seek to glorify God. We do not worship to "get blessed." It just so happens, however, that God does bless us through worship. Thank God for that! Our motive is purely to praise and adore Him. As we do this, by His infinite grace and mercy, He strengthens us and bestows His love and blessing upon us.

"But let all those who put their trust in Thee rejoice; let them ever shout for joy, because Thou defendest them; let those also who love Thy name be joyful in Thee.

For Thou, Lord, will bless the righteous; with favor will Thou compass him as with a shield."　　　　　Psalm 5:11-12

We may ask, therefore, with sincerity of heart, "Does our corporate worship edify me?" Does it give people a sense of God's love, His strength, His power? Does it affirm in this troubled world that God is in control? Does it prepare us and equip us spiritually to face what lies ahead of us in the next week? Do we feel a slight reluctance at the close of worship to leave the presence of God? Do we go out feeling warmed and alive with God's love and compassion?

Good worship, borne out of intense and passionate love for God and each other, does all of those things. We are allowed to ask, "Does our worship edify?" not because we are on a journey of self-indulgence. God forbid! We ask it because we need to know if we are missing the mark. God made us as people with feelings and emotions. True, we cannot depend heavily on them, but to deny their existence is to present an incomplete and frustrating picture of who we are. We should never imply that God has no concern for that aspect of our nature. If God does not care about our emotions and feelings then why did Jesus say, "Those things I have spoken that your joy may be full." (John 15:11) God knows exactly who we are and He ministers to our entire person, spirit-soul-and body. He knows our strengths and our weaknesses. He knows our hopes and our fears. He asks us to come into His rest. He promises to have His peace fill our souls. Does our worship affirm that? Does our worship really minister strength through its proclamation of God's nature and kingdom?

Some time ago I came in contact with a minister who really thought his role was to "challenge" the congregation into a mood of repentance. Weekly they were made to feel the weight of social injustice in society. I met very few people who left those services feeling "equipped and strengthened." Yes, we do have a responsibility to stand for justice and to reach out to the oppressed. However, this is done far more effectively if we do it out of strength derived from powerful worship which proclaims truth. A compassionate heart inspired by the power of the Holy Spirit, moving in the will of God, can do great things against staggering odds. A guilty heart wincing from the piercing blows of some sort of spiritual "brow-beating" can do very little. The hopeless and oppressed are looking for strength to grasp. The wicked need to be confronted with the truth of the Gospel proclaimed in power. We manifest these things by spending quality time in God's presence, bathed in His word. Yes, our worship must edify! Let us not be bashful about confessing that we are strengthened and guided through abandoning ourselves to worshipping the living God!

"I will love Thee, O Lord, my strength.
The Lord is my rock, and my fortress, and my deliverer; my God, my strength, in whom I will trust; my shield, and the horn of my salvation, and my high tower.

I will call upon the Lord, Who is worthy to be praised," . . .   *Psalm 18:1-3*

FRUIT

Does our worship bear fruit? Are lives changed? Are proud spirits broken? Are shallow streams deepened? Are Christian brothers and sisters moved to deeper commitment and to bold lives in Christ? Does our worship fill us to overflowing with God's love, kindness, compassion? Are we filled with joy?

"Also that day they offered great sacrifices, and rejoiced; for God had made them rejoice with great joy."   *Nehemiah 12:43*

Does our worship leave us glowing with God's shining light? Through our worship are we growing in grace, knowledge, and truth? These are some tough questions. Nevertheless, our worship must bear fruit. We shall be judged on these very criteria.

"I am the true vine, and my Father is the vinedresser. Every branch in Me that does not bear fruit He takes away; and every branch that bears fruit, He purges, that it may bring forth more fruit."   *John 15:1-2*

Notice also the end result of our bearing fruit. The Father is glorified.

"In this is My Father glorified, that you bear much fruit; so shall you be my disciples."
John 15:8

As we come together, pouring ourselves out in praise and adoration of God, we grow in His nature. I know that this may sound severe, but if we do not see fruit emerging from our lives as worshippers, either our worship is misguided and misdirected or we have hardened our hearts and possibly even become a licentious people. Why is it that we keep things going for so long when it is apparent that no real fruit is being produced? We need to move with God and not get our feet so firmly entrenched in the concrete of programs, activities, and schedules. Let us not be afraid to lay the axe to the root if fruit is not forthcoming. Lord, by your grace, may our lights beam brightly. May they gain their radiance from Your presence and illumine vast realms of darkness. May You be glorified.

"Let your light so shine before men, that they may see your good works, and glorify your Father, who is in heaven."
Matthew 5:16

GIFTS EMERGING

Another important benchmark in assessing our worship is whether or not gifts, talents, and abilities are emerging from and through our worship. It has been my experience that Spirit filled worship directed in truth towards God serves as a breeding ground for gifts. As people come together with an earnest zeal and commitment for the Lord, gifts start to emerge. Literary gifts, artistic gifts, musical and vocal gifts, gifts of worship, leadership gifts, ministry gifts, all of them begin to be manifested and raised up. Talent attracts talent and godliness attracts godliness. In worship this is especially true. For example, when the music is inspired, consecrated to the Lord, and quality oriented, it is remarkable how musicians and singers start appearing, wanting to take part. We must, however, continually stress discipleship and commitment. One of the goals of worship leadership must be to encourage and develop gifts and abilities that, when exercised, can bring glory to God.

I believe that we can expect to see the emergence of an entire spectrum of God's gifts resulting from a healthy church or fellowship, knit together in dynamic praise filled worship. We do not worship gifts. However, they are given to equip the body and enhance the ministry of the Church. We really need to be open to the Holy Spirit and not bound by preconception and fear. Scripture, as always, is our guide.

Ideally, we seek to manifest God's nature in our midst. This not only includes His love and mercy, but also His glory and power. May it be said of our ministry, "They have preached the Gospel to the poor, they have brought healing to the sick in Jesus' name, they have preached deliverance to the captives, and recovering of sight to the blind, they have given new life to the broken hearted, and they have set at liberty those who are bruised. They have proclaimed in word and deed the Gospel of the Kingdom." Do gifts which edify the body and enhance our ministry emerge from our worship? . . . From our lives as worshippers?

"FIRE"

Any assessment of worship would be incomplete without this final aspect of fervent inspiration. Oh, how our churches need fire. We need preaching that stirs men's souls and moves us deeply to lasting commitments. We need music that lifts worshippers into the heavenlies and that sings forth the glory and power of God. We need prayer that is able to move mountains and bring down dominions, principalities, and powers. We need sacraments that manifest God's sovereign grace in our midst. Yes, we need the Holy Ghost and fire! Oh Lord, may our worship prepare the hearts and kindle the flames!

"Unto thee it was shown, that thou might know that the Lord, He is God; there is none else beside Him.

Out of heaven He made thee to hear His voice, that He might instruct thee; and upon earth He showed thee His great fire, and thou heardest His words out of the midst of the fire."

Deuteronomy 4:35-36

Chapter 8

LEADERSHIP

"I am the good shepherd, and know My sheep, and am known of mine.
As the Father knoweth Me, even so know I the Father; and I lay down My life for the sheep."
John 10:14-15

I am searching for words to describe just how important this topic is. To discuss worship without covering the area of leadership is like writing a book on education without ever mentioning the qualities that a good teacher must have. We have fallen down drastically in the area of leadership. In addition, a degree of distortion has crept into our perception of the functioning and role of a leader in the church. How earnestly I pray that we catch a real vision for leadership. Lord, open our hearts and our minds.

In the area of worship, and for that matter the entire ministry of the church, we need anointed leaders. We need men and women raised up by God, filled with the Holy Spirit, and with a clear vision of just who God's people are to be and what paths they are to follow. In addition, these individuals should have hearts of servants and be able to inspire, equip, and build up the Body. They should be ready and willing to "die" that the "sheep" may live.

Today, we find two classes of Christians, clergy and laity or, if you prefer, shepherds and sheep. A sort of "caste" system has developed and in many cases a huge gulf separates the two classes. As I said earlier, we need leaders. I am not talking here about doing away with leadership. That would be both unscriptural and ridiculous. We have developed, however, something here that divides the Body and that, if carried to its frequent conclusion, hinders the growth and ministry of the church.

Clergy often become a trained, professional elite whose role consists of doing all the preaching, visiting the sick, planning the worship, leading evangelism programs, leading Christian growth studies, teaching at Bible studies, leading various prayer groups, heading endless committees, acting as leader of the board, administering the sacraments, and taking care of just about anything else I forgot to put on the list! If we combine all of the functions assumed by the pastor with the large number of people under his leadership, we have an impossible situation. The results of this are often most severe on the clergy themselves. They wind up feeling frustrated, threatened, inadequate, and utterly exhausted. The solution proposed by many is to "hire more clergy." This may provide short term relief, but if the root problem is not recognized, long run complications will persist. More bases may be covered but the clergy/laity gap is deepened. Obviously, there are exceptions. There are clergy who have truly laid down their lives for the support and ministry of the church. Those men of God know what is being said. Thank God for godly leaders! Shepherds like these spread the fertile soil out of which the tender, but beautiful plant grows. Nevertheless, when one views the church in its entirety, a large scale problem is evident.

To begin with, let us look at the matter of credentials. When we hear the expressions "ordained ministry" and "lay ministry" what comes to mind? Would the Disciples make it today? They were common men. They were not well educated as a rule and there was not a religious leader among them. Jesus, in fact, seemed to purposely avoid the religious credentials of His day. Would John or Peter be given access to many pulpits today if their only claim was that they knew Jesus? Naturally, any church must use discernment in allowing others to minister, but the point here is that we have placed such emphasis on academic credentials that we have run the risk of locking the doors of ministry to people raised up by God with definite gifts.

I am for education and training; however, I ask these questions: Does knowledge automatically bring spirituality? Does a seminary diploma bestow maturity? Does training alone make a leader? Does ordination guarantee God's calling? To make the problem more lucid, consider this: What happens if a 50 year old man, who has been a pew sitter for most of his life, suddenly catches fire for God and has a definite gift for preaching? Or what if he has an anointing to pray for the sick. Or what if God sovereignly bears witness in power to his administration of the sacraments?! Do you see the complications? Should we send him off to seminary? Do you then forbid him from exercising any God given gift until he gets "official papers?" Are there really significant and meaningful avenues within your denomination or local church for this man to grow in leadership and exercise his gifts in ministry? Or do we put him in sort of a box and hope he stays contented and quiet? Why do you think that there are so many "para church" organizations springing up? Many men and women are deeply frustrated trying to grow in the Lord and to express the vision and gifts God has given them. Please do not misunderstand me. I am not against seminaries. I am, however, against any structure of ministry which narrowly defines "who is called" or "who may respond to God's call."

> *"But you are a chosen generation, a royal priesthood, a holy nation, a people of His own, that you should show forth the praises of Him who hath called you out of darkness into His marvelous light,"* 1 Peter 2:9

I have heard this scripture read and expounded upon in "high" churches and in "free" churches. I have seen clergy in robes and vestments and also ones in business suits address themselves to this scripture. (It also appears in the Old

Testament—Exodus 19:6) Do we really believe it? Is it working in our setting? I think that we often want lay people to "get turned on" and become quite involved in church functions and activities, but we are threatened by any gifts or abilities any might have which tread on an exclusive area of ordained ministry. God have mercy on us if we are holding people back for fear of losing authority or position. A leader should feel a genuine calling or burden to bring his flock into maturity. For what purpose? To exalt his ministry or to sit admiringly at his feet? Of course not. He should fervently desire to inspire, train, and equip the saints to seize the world for Christ! To proclaim the kingdom of God!

I know of a man who sold his business and offered to be of help to his church in any needed ministry area. To make a long story short, he was kept on a very short leash. This was not because he was pushy or inexperienced; but rather, it was thought that his involvement in certain areas was "not lay ministry." He was later replaced by another clergy. Lord help us if we are playing games with true ministry.

Jesus said, "As thou hast sent me into the world, even so have I also sent them into the world." (John 17:18) Do you think the Disciples could have or would have done the work they were to do if Jesus had remained with them? If He had continued with them in the flesh? There comes a rewarding yet very painful moment with any leader when he must decrease so that others may increase. Are we willing to do that? Like the grain of wheat that falls into the ground, are we willing to die so others may bring forth much fruit? Or are we possessive about our leadership role or position? Do we clutch onto that blessed authority given to us in our leadership role? Do we inwardly love and covet the praise of men? Do we somehow enjoy feeling "exalted?" (Lay leaders, just to set the record straight, are not exempt from the above questions!) Is there a flash of soulish pride that streaks across one's heart when someone says, "Reverend," "Pastor," or "Father?"

I once heard a story related about a man who wanted to go to a seminary but never quite was able to do it. The point of the story was to show that we need to be steadfast in our calling. What emerged, however, was a mild implication that this man missed the highest calling, ordained ministry, and therefore had to settle for "other areas of service." Is that how we really feel? Are there two classes of Christians? I believe that it would grieve God terribly if we were really to promote two types of believers; professionals (bearing official seals of approval) and non or semi-professionals (of questionable status and credentials.)

Recently I read of a minister who had come to a point of crises in his life. His ministry seemed to be going nowhere in particular. His church was failing financially and in other areas. He finally made the decision to "lay it all down." He decided to quit trying to be the "priest" to the people and to merely be their brother. What a revelation! God at that point began giving his ministry back to him in very profound ways. Do we not believe that anything given up in love and obedience to Christ will come back a hundred fold?

"And every one that hath forsaken houses, or brethren, or sisters, or father, or mother, or wife, or children, or lands, for My name's sake, shall receive an hundredfold, and shall inherit everlasting life.

But many that are first shall be last, and the last shall be first." —Matthew 19:29-30

I have listened to some clergy share about how they wear "masks" in front of their congregations. They fear that by getting too close some weakness will be spotted. Some live with the constant threat of being recognized for the people they really are, flaws and all. Many of these same clergy feel they can only "be open" with other clergy. Their relationship to parishiners must be "professional." How tragic it is not to be able to share freely and support one another in love.

The class mentality is not limited to the ordained. I remember some time ago a particular city where God was sovereignly beginning to move. A vision for Body ministry was emerging. What happened? It was suddenly decided that all of the leaders should get together. (Actually, this is a very positive idea.) A "shepherd's conference" was called and, although this was by no means the intention, a distinction emerged between shepherds and sheep. Then, there was the question of what shepherds were really the leaders in the city. And so it went. I do not think the move of the Spirit got much past that point. I suppose that leadership is something that we all have a tendency to get "in the flesh" about.

We need to let God raise up leaders. In addition, we must not be afraid to allow other Christians to step out in ministry. "What if they blow it?" "What if they say the wrong thing?" Well, we need to exercise loving discernment, but beyond that, we have a calling to bring our sheep into maturity. If they stumble, we will be there to pick them up. What father would not want his son to grow into maturity. Sure, there are times when in faith we have to take risks. Eventually the son drives the car, alone, for the first time. Other responsibilities are entrusted to him. Then, he becomes a mature, responsible adult capable of functioning in the world. So should it be in the church. It is unnatural to keep "spiritual children" dependent on their "spiritual fathers." We teach them, we love them, we help them to grow. Then, we must trust them with real responsibility, not phony responsibility. (Son, I have something very important for you to do. Yes, dad, what is it? Go upstairs and bring down my slippers, please!) We can do that same thing spiritually and it is destructive.

Our worship can be smothered under a blanket of authoritarian, self-protective leadership. We need to come before God humbly and together as a body. If we can really learn to share together in deep bonds of trust and sacrificial love, our personal roles will seem insignificant. And yet, after we give up our precious positions, the Lord is free to raise up truly powerful gifts and abilities under the direction and anointing of the Holy Spirit. All who travel this road find that their sense of personal achievement, now surrendered on the altar of sacrifice, is strangely fulfilled in a much deeper manner.

"So the last shall be first, and the first last; for many are called, but few chosen."

Matthew 20:16

What then is a leader? A leader is one raised up by God with abilities and gifts which can equip, strengthen, and edify the Body. God has ordained leadership, not anarchy. In any body of believers gifts and abilities will emerge if we allow the Holy Spirit to move and work. A leader, furthermore, has the heart of a servant. He does not seek to protect or exalt his position, but lives and sacrifices to see others grow to maturity and succeed. A leader not only lives and ministers in the spirit of Christ, he ministers Christ. People who come in contact with him witness Christ's presence shining through.

In order for Christ's light to shine through clearly, brokenness must exist. This does not mean that the leader is passive and devoid of strength and personality. Indeed, our unique God-created personalities come to fruition when transformed in the image of Christ. We still remain unique individuals. Also, to be broken does not mean that one does not stand boldly for truth. A broken individual stands on guileless ground when he proclaims the Lord's message.

Leadership also has vision. Knowledge must be present in regard to God's will for the flock. A revelation of God's family, the Body of Christ is necessary. Who are we to be? Where are we to go? What are we to do? We are a family joined together by bonds of love and devotion. The strong help the weak. There is common purpose, and a common expression and experience of life. There is also understanding and trust.

Leadership must also recognize and overcome "sheep mentality." You see, much of the problem of Christian class distinction stems from the "laity." I have met many lay people who want to do nothing except be led. Others attend countless Bible studies, run off to conferences, listen to various speakers passing through town, watch a full schedule of Christian TV, and yet never desire to stand up and minister in Christ's name. It is as though exposure to Christian teaching and the absorption of Bible knowledge are ends in themselves. They never seek to apply "the knowledge" in ministry. When Christians cherish and foster this "sheep" mentality, they are asking for a domineering form of leadership.

Earlier, I referred to a father-son relationship. As I watch my boys romping in the yard, I realize that they enjoy being children, but God's will is that they grow into adulthood. My role as a parent is to see that this process takes place in a healthy manner. The role of a Christian leader is to see that spiritual children also grow into maturity. It may take patience, discipline, encouragement, trust, and risks. Leadership recognizes and overcomes "sheep" mentality.

Christian leaders, finally, should train their flock to be worshippers. This is a sovereign calling and responsibility. A leader, therefore, must first be a worshipper himself. He must be sensitive to the voice and leading of the Holy Spirit. He must know what it means to go into God's presence in "holiness." He must know what it means to intercede and travail before God in holy fear. He needs to have experienced both God's grandeur, majesty, and power in his life and also, God's loving, chastening discipline. Out of those peaks and valleys come brokenness, strength, and maturity. He must know what it means to venture with God in faith, to overcome fear and doubts, to trust God amidst adversity, and to pass through the fire clinging on to the Lord's hand.

A leader is able to lovingly worship with others. He is able to teach others how to draw near to God. He is able to instill a burning desire in others for God. He is rooted in the purposes of God. He is able to bring out and recognize those gifts which enhance worship and the ministry of the Body. He builds up and supports, but he does not dominate. He is a brother, not a manipulator or dictator. He is filled with the Holy Spirit and able to teach others to receive God's power in their lives. He is able to lead his flock in humble, loving obedience. Do you question why leadership is essential to worship?

Dear Lord, raise up strong, godly leaders for your people!

"And whosoever will be chief among you, let him be your servant;

Even as the Son of man came not to be ministered unto, but to minister, and to give His life a ransom for many."

Matthew 20:27-28

"Jesus said unto him, 'Feed My sheep.'"

John 21:15-17

Chapter 9

IMPLEMENTING AND ENHANCING WORSHIP/MUSIC

"Oh, come, let us sing unto the Lord; let us make a joyful noise to the rock of our salvation.

Let us come before His presence with thanksgiving, and make a joyful noise unto Him with psalms.

For the Lord is a great God, and a great King above all gods.

In His hand are the deep places of the earth; the strength of the hills is His also.

The sea is His, and He made it, and His hands formed the dry land.

Oh, come, let us worship and bow down; let us kneel before the Lord our maker.

For He is our God, and we are the people of His pasture, and the sheep of His hand. Today if you will hear His voice, . . ."   Psalm 95:1-7

Music is a vital part of worship. When God touches people or performs great works in their behalf, they break into songs of praise! A heart filled with joy and praise cannot help singing to the Lord.

"Speaking to yourselves in psalms and hymns and spiritual songs, singing and making melody in your heart to the Lord."

Ephesians 5:19

Scriptures are flooded with references to praising God in song and with instruments.

"Praise Him with the sound of the trumpet; praise Him with the psaltery and harp.

Praise Him with the timbrel and dance; praise Him with stringed instruments and flutes.

Praise Him upon the loud cymbals; praise Him upon the high sounding cymbals.

Let everything that hath breath praise the Lord. Praise ye the Lord." Psalm 150:3-6

That lays it down pretty completely doesn't it! As far back as I can remember, music has played an integral part in my life. (Can I help it if I am biased?) Nevertheless, stated as humbly as I can, music seems to be absolutely essential to the expression and fulfillment of God's people in responding to and communing with Him. God has given us music as a marvelous gift of worship. What a wondrous blessing it is! What, then, should we strive for in our worship music?

QUALITY

We discussed the concept of quality in worship earlier. It has particular application to our music. I am continually surprised at the lackluster attitude of musicians and choir members in regard to worship. Frequently, music is sung or played out of personal skill and expertise. Dedication, practice, and inspiration are lacking. Church musicians need to be acutely aware of their important role in worship leadership. Musicians, we are not just playing songs, we are standing before God in worship! A musician or choir member must be a worshipper in order for their music to "sing out to God." We need deep commitments to prayer and practice. To neglect either area is to offer God inferior consecration.

Our function as pastoral musicians is to facilitate and enhance the family of God in worship. We are not presenting a music appreciation class! We are not there to do our own thing or to be exalted and "recognized." First, we must thoroughly know the music, internalize it, and be sensitive in its performance. How often we sing words without ever realizing what we are proclaiming. Also, we frequently sing or play music without a real sensitivity to the expression of corporate worship taking place and the voices blending all around us.

Some practical items: Make sure that all of the instruments are in good playing condition. Some of those church pianos are terrible! Or what about that guitar which has not had a new set of strings in several years! The list could go on and on. Next, tuning is essential. There is no comparison with the sound of a good instrument properly tuned. Guitars and stringed instruments especially need to allow sufficient time to tune up accurately with the piano or organ. We need to listen continually to make certain that we stay in tune during the entire worship service. Let us not attempt to praise God in a haphazard fashion.

Our rehearsals need to be worship experiences. How much better we play and sing and how much greater is the inspiration with which we perform if our rehearsal time is not merely practice, but genuine worship. All participants must make a commitment to this. One or two insensitive "busybodies" can destroy a meaningful worship rehearsal. A choir that prays together and is unified in the spirit and in the vision of its ministry of worship will sing much better! Furthermore, there is that wonderful intangible quality that emerges from people singing and playing out of hearts filled with intense love for the Lord. Let us make firm commitments to offer God absolutely the very best.

SENSITIVITY

After commitment to quality comes the development of sensitivity. Any piece of music can be destroyed, not only by a faulty performance, but also by a cold, dispassionate interpretation. Sensitivity involves what music we select, when it is to be used, and how it is interpreted. We must be aware of what the Holy Spirit is saying in regard to the nature or character of God being proclaimed and in regard to the manner in which we are corporately worshipping Him. Are we at this point worshipping in a mood of quiet awe or holy stillness? Are we triumphantly affirming His power and might? Sensitivity is a beautiful thing. We learn to listen to each other and to respond to and compliment expressions and feelings as they emerge. (Isn't that what much of our Christian life is about?)

It is quite possible for an entire congregation to develop musical sensitivity. When this happens, worship becomes a wonder to behold. The people of God, together and as one voice, rise and swell with the inspiration of the Holy Spirit. The key lies in one word, "LISTEN." Listening is something of a lost art. We need to be able to respond to what we are hearing. We must each grasp the feeling and mood and the vision of what is transpiring. With zeal tempered by a sensitive spirit, we then join in with voice, heart, and soul.

APPROPRIATENESS

This is closely related to sensitivity. How something is interpreted may change as the worship experience unfolds. For example, we may play or sing a piece of music boldly or majestically at one point in the service and interpret it or a very similar piece lyrically and quietly later on. The music we select and the manner in which it is played or sung must be appropriate to the place at which it occurs, the message being emphasized, and the general mood being created by the Holy Spirit. Many different styles of music may be appropriate in general to worship, but the application, interpretation, and execution need to be infinitely sensitive. Musicians and singers need to be sensitive to the Holy Spirit. They must learn to hear His gentle voice. They must sense His presence in the unfolding drama of worship. He is here! It is an exciting thing to worship God through music. We must make certain that our hearts and spirits (and also our eyes and ears) are right with God. Remember, we are not putting on a concert! We are worshipping the living God, holy and mighty, with music and song.

Finally, each and every piece of music has a message and character, a range of feelings and expression, and great creative possibilities for color and texture. As the Spirit leads, explore those avenues. Make each selection an experience on the journey to the summit, an experience directly related in all ways to what has gone before and what is to come.

ECLECTIC, MEANINGFUL, RELEVANT

Music must be singable or playable and meaningful to the people. The artistic challenge is to create and select music which is powerful and poignant in content and expression, but which can readily be sung and understood by the people. This criterion has nothing to do with any particular musical style, but concerns all styles and all periods. Contemporary does not necessarily mean understandable and meaningful. In fact, in the total unfolding worship experience, it might mean the opposite and have detrimental effects if it is not appropriate to the worship taking place or performed with delicacy and sensitivity. Traditional does not mean spiritual or meaningful. Just because something is in the official hymnbook does not mean it will in any way enhance or contribute to the worship experience.

We should strive for musical richness and for a full palette of color, texture, and style. I received a letter from a pastor the other day which pointed out the errors into which we fall. He indicated that in order to freely "sing melodies unto the Lord" his congregation used no musical instruments. You see, in the name of "freedom" or "spirituality" we can really put ourselves in a box. Yes, there are times when the exact thing we should do is sing without instruments. There are other times when we should "praise God with everything that has breath!" Both of these extremes could possibly occur during the same service! How foolish it is to limit ourselves with preconceived dogma. How tragic it is to inhibit the praises of God's people. The use of only certain styles of music or only certain combinations of instruments severely limits our ability to express ourselves. God is so magnificent, creative, and diverse that we should gladly use everything possible to praise Him! Once again, the criteria for usage are quality, sensitivity, and appropriateness.

We must ardently strive for participation. God wants His people to worship. He is not really interested in having our handiwork or craftsmanship admired. We, as musicians and singers, are an integral part of the corporate vision for worship and ministry. Our responsibility is substantial. Music is a vital part of the vision of the gathered Body of Christ. Therefore, we need to be quite aware of the mandate to bring the flock into maturity. This also includes the ability to praise

God acceptably in music. Quality and sensitivity are within the grasp of everyone. Let us reach out and teach, equip, and support.

As mentioned earlier, we must use music that can be understood, grasped, and shared by the people. This does not mean that we bring in secular influences. I am firmly against that trend. We need music that inspires the worshippers and sends them into singing heart-felt praises to God. No one style of music has a corner on holiness. However, it is quite possible that a particular style of music is able to reach and move your group of people more than another. We must beware of limiting our family of worshippers to our own preferences and prejudices. (I have grown so much in my appreciation of different types of music. Earlier, when I had "definite" and "fixed" tastes, I was so limited.) To say that one particular style of music is preferable and "spiritual" is to display a rather blinding arrogance.

I heard from a choir director the other day who would not consider using anything but the finest of classics in "his" church. "Heaven forbid!" I am certain that "his" congregation was being "educated" weekly by him. Also, I have spoken with many young people who sarcastically write off any music that does not have that contemporary, top-forty, driving sound that is so popular on many Christian radio stations. Once again, both positions are in error and are missing the glorious diversity available to God's people.

We must also make certain that the participation invoked by the music is really glorifying the Lord. In this regard, allow me to share several incidents. Three of us were giving a workshop dealing with worship. At one point we led the gathering in several joyful, exhuberant numbers. The people rejoiced. In fact, without saying a word to each other, we all sensed that the rejoicing was too exhuberant. All of us sensed a sort of boisterous, raucus spirit creeping in. As a result we quickly led them in a quieter, more praise oriented piece. The mood changed and a glorious spirit of worship surfaced. We were back on track.

I also recall many incidents of leading gatherings in song only to hear a loud, boisterous, "shouting" of the lyrics. This has usually occurred in very informal settings when music was used as a background for cleaning tables or to buy time until the speaker arrived. This type of setting does not glorify the Lord. Never divorce music from an awareness of being in a worship environment.

I have shared in music in countless prayer meetings and fellowships. No two are the same. I have learned the hard way to be sensitive to the Holy Spirit. "Maybe this time we should start with subdued, reverent numbers. Perhaps we should begin with joyful, hand clapping songs of praise. Maybe we should sing some gentle songs of healing and reconciliation within the body. Perhaps we are not ready to sing at all." In this case we might need to spend time in prayer, uniting our spirits and humbling ourselves before the Lord. I have been in meetings where the singing had little or no feeling. We stopped and entered into prayer. Then, after a season of waiting on the Lord, we, again, began to sing. The difference was as night and day. After prayer, people, in song, poured out their hearts to the Lord! There is no one fixed formula. Listen to the Holy Spirit's loving voice.

USE OF FOLK INSTRUMENTS

I find this to be a real key in building meaningful worship. It has been said that in Evangelical churches there are only two acceptable instruments, organ and piano. In Liturgical churches there often is only one, pipe organ. Must we really limit God like that? Can we sense the beauty and richness possible through the use of many different instruments? In reading the Old Testament and particularly the book of Psalms, I get the feeling of a joyful and colorful assortment of instrumentation used to praise God. Why do we limit ourselves? Imagine the beauty that can result from the use of such instruments as a dulcimer, recorder, autoharp, guitar, mandolin, or various percussion instruments such as finger cymbals, tambourine, triangle, and Latin percussion. (I also encourage the use of an exciting range of band and orchestral instruments.) Folk instruments seem to have a genuine ability to speak to the people in a very personal way. I recall attending a fellowship meeting one evening and listening to a young woman sing a beautiful, haunting sort of melody while she accompanied herself on the dulcimer.

As a guitarist, I am keenly aware of the diversity of sound and style inherent in that particular instrument, and I am also aware of the need, as with any other instrument, for quality, sensitivity, and good taste. I am absolutely convinced that we can expect to see a blossoming of exciting, creative worship making joyful and skillful use of a wealth of instrumentation (folk instruments included!). When we talk about this in workshops, it gives me great pleasure to see the wide-eyed, surprised expressions on people's faces upon hearing the range of sound and harp-like timbre obtained by combining, for example, a 12-string accoustic guitar, an autoharp, and possibly a 6-string guitar. (If you add a mandolin to this, you have an extraordinary timbre.) Ears also perk up at the "lift" a piece of music can receive from the sensitive application of a variety of rhythm instruments. Praise God for richness and diversity of sound. Lord, open our eyes and ears. Enlarge our borders. Expand our horizons that we may continually worship You more fully!

START SMALL

People have asked me how to begin gaining diversity and flexibility in instrumentation. I always say, "Start small." If you have only one guitarist, for example, work with him or her in practice to gain the desired feeling of blend and interpretation. Time should also be spent working on musicianship, style, and intonation. Next, pieces should be selected which are comfortably within the reach of the musician and which can be edifying in a worship setting. Remember, you are developing and bringing out a ministry in someone. Be patient and loving. It is worth the time and effort! You will be amazed how interest, participation, involvement, dedication, and musicality start to build! I have experienced this and seen it work.

Another avenue which is prevalent today is that of pre-recorded backgrounds. Because of the growing use of this medium, it needs to be discussed. Frankly, I am not an advocate of it. I have often said that I would much rather sit with one or two people and worship God with an autoharp, guitar, or whatever, than stand in a large church with a "canned cast of thousands." I am stating my personal preference. Some may disagree, but I feel I must be honest.

Recently, a friend and I attended a demonstration session on pre-recorded music. This was the ultimate application! We entered a darkened sanctuary while background music was oozing through the elaborate sound system. Suddenly, a bombastic choral and orchestral arrangement of "O Worship

The King" sounded. At the same time a screen dropped down and the words to the song were flashed against idyllic nature scenes. When this ended, a powerful male voice started reading a Psalm (a pre-recorded voice, that is, and accompanied by a symphonic musical score). The words to the Psalm were flashed on the screen with a background picture of gorgeous mountains. All while this was going on, I kept looking around wondering, "Are there any people here? I mean, any real people?" No thanks!

We need to enter into real worship with real people and to give honor and praise to an authentic, living, present God. We also must be able to be "live" in the flow of the Holy Spirit. Lord, give us "live" worship! How would you feel if you went to church some Sunday morning, sang a few songs, said a few prayers, and then heard a voice coming over the sound system saying, "Pastor Smith could not attend today so instead of his usual message, we will broadcast a tape of well known evangelist "Ziggy Schultz!" The tape will run for 20 minutes and will be accompanied by appropriate music and pictures of nature." My case rests . . . .

HIRING PROFESSIONALS

This is another controversial subject. Generally, I am not in favor of it. Worship is sacred. It is a holy experience sanctioned by a holy and sovereign God. Music is a ministry, a powerful one. Everyone involved in this ministry needs to be committed to the Lord and to God's people. I do not, however, wish to be legalistic. There are dedicated Christians who are professional musicians and we should not hesitate to use them. You see, the problem is this: the use of professional musicians (who may not be Christians) just like the use of pre-recorded backgrounds stems from an emphasis on performance. Worship becomes viewed as a performance or a production, (albeit a professional one). The roles quickly become audience/performer. We run the risk of presenting religious entertainment, not authentic worship.

Recently, I heard a man give a talk on arranging music for use with instruments and choir. He heartily recommended using professional musicians to "spice up and enliven the service." He added that having a musician play in church was a good witness to that individual.

My response to that is twofold. First, are we that bankrupt in gifts and abilities that we must indiscriminately bring in anyone to "help us out?" Second, worship is a holy experience, shared by the body of Christ in response to the revelation and working of God in their lives and in their loving relationships with each other. It is not really supposed to be an evangelism program for lost musicians.

In this discussion it was also pointed out that due to certain musician's union regulations in certain areas, someone from the union hall might have to serve as "booker" or employer and hire the musicians for us. Do you feel comfortable with that? This may be controversial, but as a pastoral musician, I feel a heavy responsibility to be sensitive to the needs of the worshipping family and to the holiness of God.

There is definitely a rift between the people of God and the secular world. We, as God's people, are not to be isolated. We are to serve as lights in the darkness. We must reach out to the world and share the Gospel of the Kingdom in word and deed. One of the surest ways of fulfilling God's will for His people is to commit ourselves to vibrant, dynamic worship. The world cannot deny this. I believe that we are on shaky ground if we do not take the ministry of worship seriously and the consecration of all participants and leaders to heart. God asks us to give Him our best. Let us, therefore:

". . . press toward the mark for the prize of the high calling of God in Christ Jesus."

Philippians 3:14

Quality, richness, diversity, creativity, passionate consecration of heart, diligence, sensitivity, joy . . . may our musical harvest be plentiful . . . may it glorify God!

Chapter 10

THE BLOSSOMING OF THE ARTS

When hearts are on fire for God and when a vision for being a people of worship is grasped, we can expect to see a blossoming of creativity expressed toward God.

ART

The possibilities of creative use of art gifts in worship are many. Art has the unique ability to put into actual visual images the nature of God and our response to Him. I remember seeing a painting of Jesus seated in a small wood room. People were lined up to see Him (beggars, children, sick, blind). As He sat and saw them one by one, He had a look of compassion in His eyes I shall never forget. The name of the artist escapes my memory, but, that picture remains imbedded clearly. I have always wished that I was more artistic. Art gives us so many possibilities for expression.

I have sat for hours and watched my children "create" something. They become totally involved and completely absorbed. And, when finished, they have such pleased expressions. Their creation says something they really want to express and it reflects who they are. Art is a very personal medium. There is a blessed intimacy about it. I have been in churches that possessed a jubilant, festive feeling due to the creative use of banners and paintings. Other churches use very creative works of art which reflect the vision of the congregation on things such as bulletin covers, newsletters, etc. The possibilities are many and varied.

The style of art is secondary in importance. The main factors to consider are these: Does it arise out of a clear conception of truth? Does it accurately portray God or His people? It should be created with a definite sense of God's holiness. It should not originate from the secular idolization of man found in modern society. God is positive. There is a wholeness and unity about God which should pervade the arts. God has filled the earth with His beauty. His power, magnitude, compassion, and love are broader than our imaginations can perceive. A truly great range of possibilities, therefore, lies before the artist.

Once again, we must stress the consecration of the artist. It is one thing to create something to be displayed in a gallery. It is quite another, though, to offer our creative works to God. We must bow before the majesty of God, and our works must reflect His Lordship in our lives.

Again, we come to the familiar standard of quality. As with music, we absolutely must offer God the very best of our efforts. He knows the intent of our heart. Art created for use in worship should edify and bring to our hearts the message God is speaking to us. Art does speak loudly. It leaves lasting impressions and images. I feel that we can expect to see new styles of expression surface in Christian art. These new contributions will arise out of hearts totally yielded to God, refined in the community of saints, and expressed in passionate worship to our Creator.

LITERARY GIFTS

I am excited about some of the new, creative poetry and writings that are beginning to emerge. Not only can dramatized readings be used effectively, but beautiful, sensitive, and poignant poetry can instill a mood and bring forth a message. We should choose our words sensitively. We should use them wisely and artistically. Some churches encourage members to share their faith in writings which appear in bulletins and newsletters. This is a good way to bridge gaps and bring the body closer together. When readings are to be used in worship, careful selection is needed and conscientious rehearsal is required.

Literary gifts are able to reflect, in vivid verbal pictures, the depth of joy and heart rendering trials, fears, and sadness we encounter along our paths. These gifts allow us to share, to communicate.

I told the participants in a workshop once that there seems to be something inside of each of us trying to cry out in full expression of heart to God. That is part of our experience as

Christians and of walking with our Lord. Literary gifts allow us to do just that. They speak clearly to each other and to God about what is in our heart. Quality, sensitivity, consecration, creativity, . . . let the gifts flow!

DANCE, INTERPRETIVE MOVEMENT, WORSHIPPING GOD WITH OUR BODIES

This is a very exciting area. Finally, we are coming out of gross inhibitions and into a holy liberty with regard to using our bodies. For a long time we have talked about worshipping God with our hearts, souls, bodies, but we have been "fudging" on the last one. Just let someone lift their hands to the Lord and crisis prevails in the church! We all know the validity scripturally for the laying on of hands, but have we considered the use of this part of our anatomy in worship?

"Thus will I bless Thee while I live; I will life up my hands in Thy name."

Psalm 63:4

"Lift up your hands in the sanctuary, and bless the Lord."   *Psalm 134:2*

"Let my prayer be set forth before Thee as incense; and the lifting up of my hands, as the evening sacrifice."   *Psalm 141:2*

> *"I stretch forth my hands unto Thee; my soul thirsts after Thee, like a thirsty land."*
>
> Psalm 143:6

> *"I will, therefore, that men pray everywhere, lifting up holy hands, without wrath and doubting;"*
>
> 1 Timothy 2:8

Or, consider this usage of the hands.

> *"Oh, clap your hands, all ye peoples; shout unto God with the voice of triumph."*
>
> Psalm 47:1

What about kneeling? Is there anything wrong with getting on our knees in prayer and worship?

> *"Let us kneel before the Lord our Maker."*
>
> Psalm 95:6

> *"And when they were come to the multitude, there came to Him (Jesus) a certain man, kneeling down to Him, and saying, Lord, have mercy on my son; . . ."*
>
> Matthew 17:14-15

> *"But Peter put them all forth, and kneeled down, and prayed; . . ."*
>
> Acts 9:40

"For this cause I bow my knees unto the Father of our Lord Jesus Christ,"

Ephesians 3:14

"That at the name of Jesus every knee should bow, . . ." *Philippians 2:10*

Or, to carry it one step further:

"Let us worship and bow down;"

Psalm 95:6

"and the four and twenty elders fell down before the Lamb, . . ." *Revelation 5:8*

"And all the angels stood round about the throne, and about the elders and the four living creatures, and fell before the throne on their faces, and worshipped God." *Revelation 7:11*

The point is this: we must overcome the notion that to be spiritual is to deny the body. For a long time we have harbored the notion that the body is somehow bad and that movement of the body, even something as simple as lifting hands, is ugly and fleshly. Instead, we must affirm that the body is the temple of the Holy Spirit, and there is beauty and grace in worshipping God with our bodies. To deny the use of the body in worship is similar to trying to put air into a balloon which cannot be expanded. Stand, sit, kneel, arms uplifted, arms extended and reaching out, arms crossed over chest, head bowed, head uplifted, eyes closed, eyes opened . . . let us not be legalistic or inhibited about our bodies in worship. Scriptures have many accounts of people worshipping God with their bodies. This even includes dancing.

"And Miriam the prophetess, the sister of Aaron, took a timbrel in her hand; and all the women went out after her with timbrels and with dances."   *Exodus 15:20*

"Let them praise His name in the dance; . . ."   *Psalm 149:3*

"Praise Him with the timbrel and dance; . . ."   *Psalm 150:4*

Yes, out of exhuberant joy for the Lord, David even danced. (2 Samuel 6:16-23) Even the New Testament has its share of leaping for joy.

"And he, leaping up, stood and walked, and entered with them into the temple, walking, and leaping, and praising God."   *Acts 3:8*

We need to expand our thoughts on creative ways to use our bodies in worship to bring glory to God.

"I beseech you therefore, brethren, by the mercies of God, that you present your bodies a living sacrifice, holy, acceptable unto God, which is your reasonable service."

Romans 12:1

Interpretive movement or symbolic dance is an extremely beautiful experience to behold. It has deep spiritual meaning for young and old. The congregation, together, interprets the song with flowing gestures and symbols. It leaves a significant and lasting impression upon one's spirit. I remember the feeling of beauty and holy awe that filled me when I first saw a congregation join in a beautiful song of praise and express the words in movement. Their hands, arms, and bodies seemed to flow with divine grace as the gentle melody of praise was sung. Even the children took part. I was deeply moved by this sight.

Since then, we have introduced simple interpretive movement in workshops. Our experience has been that a feeling of release takes place. It is like finding new, meaningful words to use in praising God. I cannot begin to express how significant interpretive movement is to children. They love it, it speaks to them, they understand it, it is their language. (They still enjoy expressing themselves with their bodies. We adults have to relearn how enjoyable and meaningful it can be!)

We worship God in reverence and holiness, but let us worship Him freely. Let us not be afraid to express ourselves with our bodies. The fuller our hearts become, the more we shall break forth into new and significant avenues of worship.

"For ye are bought with a price; therefore, glorify God in your body and in your spirit, which are God's."   1 Corinthians 6:20

ARCHITECTURE

It is necessary to include a word here about architecture. Architecture not only boldly proclaims our view of God and what worship should be, it also can greatly enhance or hinder it. Briefly, architecture should reflect our vision of being united together as a family of God's people. It should facilitate worship and increase the sense of participation and involvement. It should diminish the distinction between performer and audience and affirm the fact of being co-participants joined together in common objective.

At this point, I would also like to offer a personal plea for good acoustics. We have carpeted our sanctuaries and padded our pews so heavily that we cannot seem to worship without elaborate and expensive sound systems. (Lord, help us if the power goes off!)

My family attended worship recently at a new church. The sanctuary was quite small. At best it could seat only a few hundred people. We were seated only about 30 feet from the pulpit and yet, without the sound system, it was difficult or impossible to hear what was being said. Good acoustics give us great flexibility. It is difficult to ever have spontaneity in worship if we have to use a microphone at all times to be heard.

Lighting is also a subject that I am "somewhat of a nut on!" I like light. Let us at least have the flexibility to create a joyful atmosphere with good lighting. Another factor to consider is the spacing of the pews. Frequently they are so close together that kneeling is forever impossible.

We also need to keep a keen eye on allowing meaningful involvement and participation in Holy Communion. Many churches celebrate this Sacrament far too seldom. In addition to yielding access to God's grace in a significant manner and fostering a genuine sense of community, I find the Eucharistic setting to be one of the greatest fertile environments for inspiration and creativity in the arts, especially music. Jesus said, "Do this in remembrance of Me." As mentioned earlier, it is remembrance and it is also celebration. Architecture should enable this Sacrament to be easily and meaningfully shared.

Be flexible! When we design and build, let us prayerfully reflect on what we want to say about God, who we are as a worshipping family, and how we express our relationships. In addition, let us gain a vision for worship in the future.

PREACHING

Preaching the word of God should be considered an art. Therefore, it needs some mention here. Like music, we need to master our technique, we need to thoroughly understand and know the "score," and we must depend on the Holy Spirit for inspiration. We cannot proclaim God's word apart from the anointing of the Holy Spirit and expect fruit to result. Also, we cannot refuse to prepare and depend on the Spirit to get us through. Much time needs to be spent in prayer prior to the preparation and delivery of the message. An inspired preacher is a worshipper. He is sensitive to the Holy Spirit and can hear "what the Spirit is saying to the church."

Moreover, the inspired teaching on God's word should

exhort and encourage, inspire and comfort. It should instill a God given vision in the very hearts of the people. It should flow in relation to the peoples' relationship to God and to each other and in the spirit of the worship experience.

We then must ask: Preachers, are you willing to lay down that prepared sermon and speak from the heart if the Spirit so directs? Are you teachable? Can you learn from "laity?" Are you seeking and listening to the Holy Spirit? Are you giving God quality time, waiting on Him, worshipping Him in private?

Preaching the word of God is a solemn responsibility. It is an important part of the way we worship. It is essential to the ministry of the church. Once again, let us offer unto God our very best.

"The words that I speak unto you, they are spirit, and they are life."   *John 6:63*

Chapter 11

ENEMIES OF WORSHIP

"Create in me a clean heart, O God, and renew a right spirit within me.

Cast me not away from Thy presence, and take not Thy Holy Spirit from me.

Restore unto me the joy of Thy salvation, and uphold me with a willing spirit."

Psalm 51:10-12

There are things that can impede our journey. Some of them serve as blockades on the road. Others are outright enemies to the purposes of God. Still others deceptively lie as detours which, when followed, lead us into a troublesome maze whose exit is difficult and uncertain. Let us then look at the things that can stifle, hinder, obstruct, and actually dry up genuine worship. It should be noted that when the Holy Spirit begins a significant move, a real breakthrough in a group of Christians, the enemy moves quickly to destory, steal, and try to stop this movement. The early stages of a real awakening of worship usually bring about a direct confrontation with one or more of the following items. Let us therefore:

"Be sober, be vigilant, because your adversary, the devil, like a roaring lion walketh about, seeking whom he may devour.

Whom resist steadfast in the faith, knowing that the same afflictions are accomplished in your brethren that are in the world."

1 Peter 5:8-9

FEAR

Fear continues to be one of the most debilitating enemies of the purposes of God. As with the Hebrews, when God shows us the promised land and then says, "Take it, it is yours!", some always come and say "But there are giants in the land!" We then must decide which voices to listen to. Fear of the Lord, as described earlier, is a blessing. Many types of fear, however, are curses. Some of these include fear of the unknown, fear of emotion, fear of religion, fear of man, and Satanic fear. People today are filled with fear and anxiety. The fears come from many directions. (Fear of nuclear war, fear of economic collapse, fear of illness, etc.) If there ever was a time when God's people need to be trusting solely in Him, it is now. I have found in my own life that fear is a cruel, harsh taskmaster. What you fear will be your master. It will come to dominate you.

Worshipping God freely and openly affirms His sovereignty and proclaims our faith in Him. It denies fear. It is only natural that fear is a key enemy which attempts to block people from experiencing the fullness of God in worship. Let us look at some of the fears referred to above.

Fear of the unknown manifests itself when we are operating in realms of insecurity. The person prone to this fear desires stability at all cost. If it comes down to it, dull routine will be chosen over spontaneous life because routine, no matter how dull, is predictable.

I once heard a pastor say that the most unspontaneous, predictable events he experienced were funerals. The most lively, filled with expectancy, were births. A person full of fear of the unknown probably would not have ventured forth with Abraham in search of a promised land. They also would have encountered great difficulty leaving Egypt with Moses. It is also doubtful whether this person would have left the wilderness, once used to it, and ventured across the Jordan River into the promised land. Fear of the unknown says, "Don't try something new, we don't know what might happen." Fear of the unknown prefers to walk by sight, not by faith.

Fear of emotion affects many of us. I have always been "guarded" with my emotions. I, like many, have reacted adversely to seeing people "get emotional" in worship. God, thankfully, has freed me in this regard. I realized one day as I looked upon someone weeping during prayer, that in a somewhat cold, detached manner I was judging them. Who are we to judge the working of God in the heart of another?

Obviously, self-control is a fruit of the Spirit, but lack of emotion is a symptom of death! God created us with feelings and emotions. How bound up we are when we are afraid to show joy or tears. Fear of emotion places a very narrow corridor in front of us. Then, it says, "Don't you dare experience God unless He comes down this very path." We become isolated from each other and separated from the fullness of His presence in worship.

We frequently run headlong into *fear of religion*. Those who are dominated by this fear tell us in rather threatening tones that if we tamper with tradition in any way, not only will our status with God be somehow in question, but the "religious powers to be" might strike us down. Generally, people filled with this fear are working out their faith in a legalistic fashion and lack real joy. Their righteousness is derived in whole or in part from compliance to written or unwritten "rules." Religion, viewed in these terms, can sap our strength and place incredibly heavy burdens upon our backs. This type of fear experiences the Holy Spirit only in "historical" terms.

Fear of man is also a frequent malady. This person is afraid of confrontation. He or she will even sacrifice truth if it looks like a smoother road. Some people will allow you to believe whatever you want so long as you keep quiet about it. Speak out what God is showing you and these individuals might "let you have it!" A person filled with fear of men will be in real bondage to those individuals waiting to "pounce"

170

upon any statement or "act of light" with which they disagree. Experience has shown me that if we move in faith in God's will concerning any crucial area, especially His purposes for the church, we will be challenged by strong personalities demanding that we stop. If we are filled with the fear of men, it is doubtful whether we will ever be able to effectively lead God's people. It is also questionable whether God's will can be fulfilled in our lives. We will be given to continuous compromise. This fear must be overcome!

Satanic fear is an irrational, dark sense of impending doom that may temporarily be experienced by someone trying amidst struggle to move on with God. It is one of Satan's nasty darts. This is an irrational fear thrown at us to scare us off course. It is designed to breed anxiety and doubt concerning God's will. In fact, it usually poses the question, "Is this really God's will?" with great frequency. Standing in faith on God's word and resisting these lies cause this fear to flee. People, however, with backgrounds in the occult, may have greater difficulty shaking this one off!

I have found fear to be like a glass barrier that makes it impossible to hear or see God. We must not yield to it. This oppressive shield can be removed only by a decision of our will based on faith in God and trust in His word. Worship breeds overcoming faith.

"For God hath not given us the spirit of fear, but of power, and of love, and of a sound mind."
1 Timothy 1:7

"Ye are of God, little children, and have overcome them, because greater is He that is in you, than he that is in the world"   1 John 4:4

TRADITION

Let me begin by saying something positive about tradition. Many of our church traditions stem from earlier, sovereign moves of God and are grounded in truth. Earlier, when talking about eclectic worship, I made the point that it is desirable to draw from the riches of worship practices both past and present. We may indeed discover that there have been elements in our traditions which have definite meaning and significance and which for some reason have been discarded or neglected. The Holy Spirit just might lead us to breathe new life into more than a few old dry bones. Suddenly, they start brimming with life. This is good and positive.

Tradition, however, can be quite destructive to true worship if it becomes an idol or if it leads to superficial, external, or hollow ritualistic practice. We must take a good hard look at what has truth and relevance in our worship and what is, in fact, "traditional religious trappings." Frequently, these trappings are passed on reverently from generation to generation, rather than the actual experience of entering God's presence. Some individuals would much prefer to stagnate the worship of God with rigid application of tradition and with an authoritarian professionalism leading to inflexible, tight controls rather than to give leeway to the Spirit's leading and the freer and more creative forms of expression and response. People who cling tenaciously to tradition may really be exhibiting one or more of the forms of fear mentioned earlier.

172

Time and time again it has been shown that if we inhibit, prohibit, or severely dampen the praise and joy-filled song of God's people, intense frustration will result. Some will remain faithful to the church, but will gradually lose their joy and enthusiasm and their ability to minister positively to others. Others will seek out any place or fellowship where they can express the desires of their hearts. Still others will tragically return to the secular world in order to try to find fulfillment.

All worship needs to conscientiously be rethought. The worship in some churches with a tradition of "freedom" and lay participation has evolved into a heirarchical form centering around a gifted or dominant pastor. On the other hand, in some of the liturgically oriented churches we have seen experimentation in form and liturgy for the sake of "experimentation" and often without vision for who God's people are and where they are to go in worship. Furthermore, in many churches we have a dogged determination to hang on to the sacred relics of tradition, irregardless of whether or not they still convey any real spiritual meaning. This is the whole point. If a particular element or practice in worship actually contributes and conveys something, it is worthy of being kept alive and renewed. If it does not, it should be discontinued. To put it more bluntly, we keep the meat and throw away the bones. Flexibility, sensitivity and discernment are needed.

IDOLS

"I am the Lord: that is My name; and My glory will I not give to another, neither my praise to carved images."　　　　　　Isaiah 42:8

173

Anything which replaces God in our hearts and minds as the object for worship is an idol. It may be something like status, recognition, social or professional position, possessions, or materialism or perhaps, it is something very dear to us like our children or spouses. (Have you ever known parents who "idolize" their children? It can lead to a domineering possessiveness and unhealthy situation.) We can also make idols of aspects of our religious faith and practice such as tradition, doctrine, liturgy, the church building, creeds, preaching, music, vestments, hymnbooks, prayerbooks, and other "sacred vessels." Finally, we may worship the idols of various social and political causes such as peace, "justice," environment, etc. As beneficial and worthwhile as any of these things might be, they cannot and must not steal our hearts. To worship an idol is to reject God. It is foolishness. It is to reject the ultimate source of all truth for something non-permanent and even false. When we begin to affirm the nature of God in worship in a powerful way, strange idols have a way of creeping up and demanding "equal time."

"Little children, keep yourselves from idols."
1 John 5:21

ARROGANT/PRIDEFUL SPIRIT

I wish this spirit were not so prevalent in religious circles. This spirit dries up fellowship and worships God on its own terms. Individuals like this frequently are quite impressed with themselves and take for granted God's infinite gratitude for the work which they do in "His behalf." Many people who strive to "be first" in religious circles live in this realm. Some educational disciplines, religious and secular, seem to foster it. A friend of mine spoke with a choir director the other day who began the conversation by reeling off his "impressive" credentials (Ph.D. in this, degrees in that.) He seemed totally absorbed with the musical expertise that he was offering the poor, uneducated populace at his church. (I am certain God was pleased and impressed!) This type of spirit cannot bow before God and cannot relate openly with others because it never has undergone brokenness at the hands of the Master. By God's grace, however, there is hope!

"God resists the proud, and gives grace to the humble."

1 Peter 5:5

"And whosoever shall exalt himself shall be abased; and he that shall humble himself shall be exalted."

Matthew 23:12

AGGRESSIVE/HARSH/STRIVING SPIRIT

Sometimes people are genuinely touched by God, their hearts are pointed towards Him, and they get a pretty good glimpse of His will for the body of Christ. Then, they go bananas! They become zealots who, with utmost insensitivity, beat to death anyone who gets in the way of "the Lord's will." They become "soldiers of the Lord" and "defenders of truth." Their intentions really are good and their zeal is genuine. The problem is that they leave a trail of wreckage behind them. In many ways I sympathize with the earnestness of these individuals. The fact remains, nevertheless, that their aggressive and insensitive spirit drives others away and keeps many from wanting to draw closer to God. They end up cramming spiritual truths into ill-timed fleshy schemes of implementation. In addition, this type of individual disrupts fellowship. In the long run, they serve as a destructive force for the carrying out of God's will.

DOMINEERING SPIRIT

This spirit seeks to define God and the Holy Spirit for everyone else. In fact, this person really may be saying, "Worship me." This is another real enemy of worship. Unfortunately, this personality type likes to hover around leadership positions. It covets them. A domineering spirit uses a wide range of skills and abilities to use, control, and manipulate people. If this does not work, he might try to brow beat them to bring them into submission. This spirit usually holds "weaker" personalities in low esteem. Christ's will is seen as conforming to "my will." A good dose of brokenness can help here; however, this spirit has a way of trying to creep back into the person from time to time.

SKEPTICISM/CYNICISM

I am from Missouri. They call it the "show me" state. Early Missouri settlers were known for their skepticism. "If you say that's true, show me!" That pretty well sums up the skeptical spirit. The only problem is that with this spirit, the person frequently does not really want to be shown. It really should read like this, "If you say that is true, show me. (but even if you show me, I'm still not going to buy it!") The skeptical spirit often has been "burned" in the past and has constructed an iron clad shield to keep from being duped or hurt in the future. This is a tragic individual. They may want to experience what God is doing, but they will not allow themselves to do it. I am reminded of the dwarfs in C.S. Lewis' book, *The Last Battle* (the final book in the Chronicles of Narnia series.) As the book ended they sat in darkness rather than acknowledge the light. They had been fooled before and no one was going to dupe them again! So, in darkness they remained. A skeptical spirit denies the Holy Spirit.

"Verily I say unto you, Whosoever shall not receive the kingdom of God as a little child, he shall not enter it."   *Mark 10:15*

Skepticism is not basic to a child's nature. They are trusting. The skeptic stands to miss out on the move of God.

Cynicism is a more bitter form of skepticism. It not only refuses to believe or to trust, it attempts to ridicule those who do. Cynicism yields bitter fruit and often denotes deep wounds in the individual.

My wife sat in worship recently behind a young couple who ridiculed much of what transpired. It was a sad experience. A cynical spirit may tread dangerously upon "the fear of the Lord." A worship leader should not yield to this enemy. He should, also, never possess this spirit! A cynical spirit attempts to judge and ridicule God and His people.

REBELLIOUS SPIRIT

This spirit hates authority and leadership. In addition, it resists discipline. It often seeks to divide in order to bring down or hurt God's leaders. It is a spirit very prevalent in the world. It seeks to do its own thing and nobody had better get in its way. When we talk of commitment to the body and to the purposes of God and when we consider bowing in submission to our Maker, we can see the difficulty this person has entering in. This individual is denying the Lordship of Christ in his or her life.

COMPLACENT/APATHETIC SPIRIT

I find this one to be the most frustrating. This person just does not seem to care one way or another. Perhaps the "heat of the sun has dried him up," or perhaps the "cares of the world have choked him." In any event, he just does not have any great degree of enthusiasm for the things of God. He may flow along, but he is probably just there for the ride.

"So, then, because thou are lukewarm, and neither cold nor hot, I will spew thee out of My mouth."
Revelation 3:16

INTELLECTUALISM

This person views everything in a cool, detached "rational" manner. He usually is also a skeptic. In any event He relates to God in a cerebral way and is dead set against anything that smells in the slightest degree like emotion. To him, God is a "gentlemen." Fair enough, but let's not make the Holy Spirit the butler. (Although we then can truly claim, "The Butler Did It!")

This individual often has a very complex personal

178

theology and because of that, rails agains affirming absolutes in regard to God's nature. There may also be a healthy dose of pride mixed in.

MURMURER/COMPLAINER

This person is a real "joy" to be around. In addition to being displeased with just about anything you do, they lie in waiting for your "big mistake." A critical spirit is present here. It finds fault, kills joy, and looks for converts to share in the misery. It usually is impossible to please this spirit because it actually enjoys being discontented. By accomodating it, you will destroy its fun. Then it will just have something else to complain about.

GOSSIP/BUSYBODY

Most churches have their share of busybodies. They keep the phone lines humming. They have the unique ability of transforming a minor problem into a major crisis by using their well-honed sense of timing and their fiendish discernment in choosing who and when to place that well chosen tidbit of information. If a family of worshippers is moving into deeper bonds of fellowship, this person can make everyone feel quite exposed with their revelations. All of us need to diligently monitor what we say!

"Out of the same mouth proceed blessing and cursing. My brethren, these things ought not so to be."

James 3:10

PROCRASTINATOR

Finally, we have the person who hears God speaking but who always seems to say, "tomorrow." How often God has a purpose for us or a blessing to bestow on us (or in someone else through us) but we deny it because we procrastinate. The word "tomorrow" must be Satan's favorite. It has often blinded individuals to God's present call and timing. When we see the cloud of God moving and do not follow it, we may lose sight of it completely. Tomorrow it may be moved to a location where a clear view from our fixed position is difficult or impossible. Regardless of the reason, we must never put off what God is saying to do today. God loves us. He is with us. If He is saying to press on, then let us stand up and do it!

Chapter 12

PRESSING ON/BREAKING INTO GLORY

"Wherefore, seeing we also are compassed about with so great a cloud of witnesses, let us lay aside every weight, and the sin which doth so easily beset us, and let us run with patience the race that is set before us."   *Hebrews 12:1*

Does it excite you to know that we are compassed about by so great a cloud of witnesses? It is as if the heavenly hosts are lined up and cheering," Press on, go for it, you can make it, it is glorious, if only you could see the finish as we see it. Press On!"

Let us think briefly of where we are going. We seek to enter and dwell in the presence of the living God, to behold His splendor and fall down in awe of His majesty. Everything inside of us wants to release itself in one heartfelt pronouncement, "Glory to God! Hallelujah!" This place is home.

God has been beckoning us to come here with Him for a long time. It is here that we will find peace and rest. The pastures are ever so green and the water is pure, clear, and strangely still. Our hearts are cleansed, our souls refreshed, and our spirits strengthened. It is here that we shall find true joy, joy that bursts forth in praise which in turn, fills us with more and more joy. It is here that we feel surrounded, enveloped by a warm radiance that melts away our fears, our worries, our cares. We drink deeply of a thirst quenching liquid that we come to know as God's love. We breathe in air that bears a vitality, a fragrance sweeter than any we have experienced. It clears our head and removes the clouds from our eyes. Oh yes, tears flow, but they are cleansing tears, tears of joy. This is the summit. God called in His gentle, but penetrating voice. We heard and followed. We persisted and overcame those things seeking to keep us from this place. Life is here. Real life. Eternity. We feel a golden chain linking us to those who have gone before. And as we look, we see that it reaches down, marking the path of those who are yet to come. We long to stay here, bathed in His luminescence. We linger, but the time has come. We know that we must leave, temporarily. We shall return, often. We know, however, that there is yet another dimension to this fullness. When we return we shall drink even deeper of these waters, for we shall journey with others. Then, He shall come in our midst. Our joy will know new heights. Our hearts will grow. They will increase in capacity to receive His love. Together we shall go forth. To endure and to triumph. To tell others, who will hear, of this place . . . of these waters. We will watch, with those clouds of witnesses we have come to know so well, as others travel to the summit on the path we have shown. We open our mouths and with saints in eternity proclaim the Divine mystery, the glorious reality: "Thy kingdom come. Thy will be done in earth, as it is in heaven."

It is worth the cost. From this summit the gospel of the kingdom can be proclaimed. It shall be heard! The roadblocks and obstacles will be there. Satan will throw his fiery darts. But, once you have seen the summit, you want to press on. God's people are learning to live in worship. What a glorious sight! The streams are flowing plentifully in the deserts and wastelands. New, beautiful plants are springing up everywhere. It is wonderful.

"The voice of rejoicing and salvation is in the tabernacles of the righteous; the right hand of the Lord doeth valiantly."   *Psalm 118:15*

It is painful to see others draw back or refuse to see. We want them to share. We know, however, that always there will be those who say, "no." Our heart grieves for them. We search our motives. Are they saying "no" because of something unseemly in us? Is there anything, O Lord, in us that is keeping them away? We go back again and again. We share in love. We communicate. Some now hear and see.

Others still say, "no." We have learned what longsuffering means. It hurts to have them stay behind. But now, we know that we must go on.

Then, there are those who seek to fight and stop this journey. The summit is not the place their heart seeks. They say and do things which surprise and wound. It is a delicate walk. We learn to listen, carefully. Sometimes we patiently say nothing. The Lord is our defense. But, there comes a time when that dove-like voice says," Stand, speak the truth, do not let my flock miss the summit!"

"Be of good courage, an He shall strengthen your heart, all ye that hope in the Lord."

Psalm 31:24

As we move on in obedience to God, we encounter much the same roadblocks that befell Nehemiah. Nehemiah, you see, was shown something by the Lord. He had a purpose and a vision. He was to rebuild the city of Jerusalem, a staggering task for a cup bearer to the king. He knew that God was with him and he set out to accomplish his task. To achieve the purposes of God, Nehemiah had to overcome ridicule (4:1-9), discouragement (4:10-23), dissention and greed or fleshly motives and ambitions (5:1-19), and scheming and plotting to distract him and throw him off course. (6:1-14) He overcame. He succeeded against terrific odds. We also will meet obstacles in doing the Lord's work. This is especially true when we try to restore power to the church. Bringing God's people into the fullness of worship will bring them into power.

Do not stagger at the mountains yet to be climbed. They may look steep and foreboding from where you are now, but

God will see that His purposes are accomplished. He does not need many to do the work. He seeks a consecrated few. Often we are the most unlikely choice. Like Gideon, the odds may seem against us and the Lord may choose to thin out our army, but if we are steadfast in His will, the mountain will be scaled. The battles are never as tough as we might think. The giants in the land are really not that big. (And they are certainly no match for the Lord!) It is worth the cost.

God is moving over the face of the earth. He is calling a people to show forth His praises. History will culminate with a mighty people worshipping God in spirit and in truth. It will be a powerful gathering. Let us be a strong people, an obedient people, a people who know and seek the glory and splendor of God, a people truly able to share His love and mercy, a people of joy, a living Body! Let us boldly and freely worship our God. The time has come.

"Then saith He unto His disciples, The harvest truly is plenteous, but the laborers are few.
Pray ye, therefore, the Lord of the harvest, that He will send forth laborers into His harvest"
Matthew 9:37-38

POSTLUDE

I have tried to do many things in this book. The attempt has been made to discuss the scriptural basis for worship, to present practical ideas for its implementation, and to provide guidelines to follow. Beyond that, I have sought to speak to your spirit and to stir in you a vision and a hunger for God's people gathered unto Him.

There are many more things that could be discussed. We could spend much time on types of prayers, forgiveness, confession, creeds, the passing of the peace of the Lord, etc. We could talk more specifically about types of worship services, forms of praise, orders of worship, and more. Worship is a broad and exciting world. Much more needs to be written in the future.

On the practical side, we are actively involved in developing and compiling new resources for use in worship. There are so many possibilities. There are so many things we can do to make worship just that much more glorious. It does not matter whether we are talking about a small home fellowship or a gathering of thousands in a huge tabernacle, church, or cathedral. With the Lord's help, we can make it better! We can bring the love of God and the joy of the Holy Spirit to the people in more meaningful ways so that we may all share more fully.

Our hearts must be steadfast. Problems always lie in the path of a servant of God. Have you ever known that not to be the case? But, time and again I have witnessed triumph through God's power and our obedience. We must remember to make worship the passion of our lives. Then, in love we must make absolutely certain that we communicate our vision, our ideas, and how we think we can walk together in unity.

We must not, however, become discouraged or deterred from our goal. Never forget this, the vast majority of God's people are crying out for meaningful, spirited worship! God is breaking through in so many places. I look around in wonder at all that He is doing. Worship is a glorious and magnificent calling. It is a blessed privilege. Let us join together in prayer that the hearts of God's people continue to catch fire throughout our land. Let us pray that our worship is so dynamic and full of life that God's sovereign power is manifestly evident in our midst. Let us pray that music and the arts explode with divine, sanctified creativity birthed and nurtured in the electrifying atmosphere of God's presence. Come, let us worship together, today!

"And blessed be His glorious name forever; and let the whole earth be filled with His glory. Amen, and Amen."   Psalm 72:19

OTHER RECOMMENDED BOOKS

1. *God's People Worship!* — A manual for building meaningful and powerful worship celebrations. (To be released in summer of 1984.)
2. *God's People Sing Alleluia!* — Glorious music for vibrant and powerful worship. A master music collection for use in all worship celebrations. (To be released in fall of 1984.)

Both books published by Mel Bay Publications.

For workshop information write: Mel Bay Publications, Inc.
#4 Industrial Dr.
Dailey Industrial Park
Pacific, MO 63069